GW00870859

The Get Up and Go Daily Planner for Busy Women 2021

ISBN 978-1-910921-53-1

Published in Ireland by
GET UP AND GO PUBLICATIONS LTD
Sligo, Ireland.
Email: info@getupandgodiary.com
www.getupandgodiary.com
Facebook: The Irish Get Up and Go Diary; Get Up and Go Events
Twitter: @getupandgo1; **Instagram:** @getupandgodiary

Compiled by: Eileen Forrestal
Graphic design: Nuala Redmond
Illustrations: Sophia Murray; dreamstime.com; shutterstock.com
Printed in Ireland by GPS Colour Graphics.

Copyright c 2007-2021 Get Up And Go Publications Ltd.

All right reserved. No part of this publication may be reproduced, stored in, or introduced into, a retrieval system, or transmitted in any form, or by any means (electronic, mechanical, scanning, recording or otherwise) without the prior permission of the Publisher. Any person who does any unauthorised act in relation to this publication may be liable to criminal prosecution and civil claim for damages.

Forgive the past – let it go
Live the present – the power of now
Create the future – thoughts become things

Dear Reader,

We are delighted that you are holding this Get Up and Go Daily Planner for Busy women 2021 in your hands today. You are about to embark on a wonderful journey. Whether you have chosen this planner for yourself or received it as a gift, we know it will provide the inspiration, motivation and empowerment you need as you progress towards fulfilling your goals and dreams in 2021.

If you would like to connect with our growing Get Up and Go community, we invite you to visit our website ***www.getupandgodiary.com*** *where you can follow our blog, find out about our new products, plus details of special offers and upcoming Get Up and Go events.*

You may also like to follow us on Facebook, Twitter or Instagram for additional words of inspiration and encouragement.

Whether you are a first time customer with Get Up and Go or you are a regular and loyal follower, we thank you and trust that you will enjoy, and benefit from, the experience. Our aim is to provide exceptional value and to continuously improve our products in line with customer demand.

If you love our Get Up and Go Diaries and Journals, we would love you to share the value with your family and friends.

Best wishes for the year ahead!

Sincerely,

Eileen, Brendan, and the Get Up and Go team

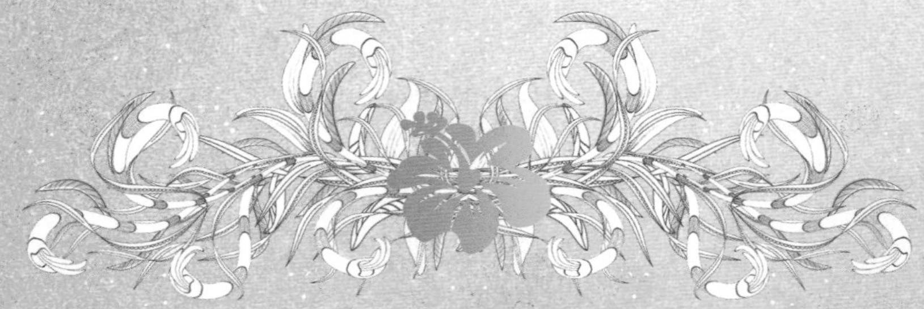

Please be advised that you can use this planner as a personal empowerment tool, and if you fill in sensitive personal details and financial records, do remember it may be seen by others. It is your responsibility to always keep your personal information private.

PERSONAL DETAILS

Name:
Address:

Nationality:

Contact details
Private:
Business:
Mobile:
Email:

Next of kin:

Blood group:
Organ donor status:
Car registration number:
Passport number:
Bank:
National insurance number:
Doctor:
Dentist:

Essential medication:
Allergies (food/drug):
Medic alert:

Facebook:
Twitter:
Instagram:
Website :

2021

January

S	M	T	W	T	F	S
					1	2
3	4	5	6	7	8	9
10	11	12	13	14	15	16
17	18	19	20	21	22	23
24	25	26	27	28	29	30
31						

February

S	M	T	W	T	F	S
	1	2	3	4	5	6
7	8	9	10	11	12	13
14	15	16	17	18	19	20
21	22	23	24	25	26	27
28						

May

S	M	T	W	T	F	S
						1
2	3	4	5	6	7	8
9	10	11	12	13	14	15
16	17	18	19	20	21	22
23	24	25	26	27	28	29
30	31					

June

S	M	T	W	T	F	S
		1	2	3	4	5
6	7	8	9	10	11	12
13	14	15	16	17	18	19
20	21	22	23	24	25	26
27	28	29	30			

September

S	M	T	W	T	F	S
			1	2	3	4
5	6	7	8	9	10	11
12	13	14	15	16	17	18
19	20	21	22	23	24	25
26	27	28	29	30		

October

S	M	T	W	T	F	S
					1	2
3	4	5	6	7	8	9
10	11	12	13	14	15	16
17	18	19	20	21	22	23
24	25	26	27	28	29	30
31						

CALENDAR

March

S	M	T	W	T	F	S
	1	2	3	4	5	6
7	8	9	10	11	12	13
14	15	16	17	18	19	20
21	22	23	24	25	26	27
28	29	30	31			

April

S	M	T	W	T	F	S
				1	2	3
4	5	6	7	8	9	10
11	12	13	14	15	16	17
18	19	20	21	22	23	24
25	26	27	28	29	30	

July

S	M	T	W	T	F	S
				1	2	3
4	5	6	7	8	9	10
11	12	13	14	15	16	17
18	19	20	21	22	23	24
25	26	27	28	29	30	31

August

S	M	T	W	T	F	S
1	2	3	4	5	6	7
8	9	10	11	12	13	14
15	16	17	18	19	20	21
22	23	24	25	26	27	28
29	30	31				

November

S	M	T	W	T	F	S
	1	2	3	4	5	6
7	8	9	10	11	12	13
14	15	16	17	18	19	20
21	22	23	24	25	26	27
28	29	30				

December

S	M	T	W	T	F	S
			1	2	3	4
5	6	7	8	9	10	11
12	13	14	15	16	17	18
19	20	21	22	23	24	25
26	27	28	29	30	31	

2021 BANK AND PUBLIC HOLIDAYS

REPUBLIC OF IRELAND
New Year's Day, 1 January; St Patrick's Day, 17 March; Good Friday, 2 April; Easter Monday, 5 April; May Day Bank Holiday, 3 May; June Bank Holiday, 7 June; August Bank Holiday, 2 August; October Bank Holiday, 25 October; Christmas Day, 25 December; St Stephen's Day, 26 December.

NORTHERN IRELAND
New Year's Day, 1 January; St Patrick's Day, 17 March; Good Friday, 2 April; Easter Monday, 5 April; May Day Holiday, 3 May; Spring Bank Holiday, 31 May; Orangemen's Holiday, 12 July; Summer Bank Holiday, 30 August; Christmas Day, 25 December; Boxing Day, 26 December.

ENGLAND, SCOTLAND AND WALES
New Year's Day, 1 January; Good Friday, 2 April; Easter Monday, 5 April; St George's Day, 23 April May Day Holiday, 3 May; Spring Bank Holiday, 31 May; Summer Bank Holiday, 30 August; Remembrance Sunday, 14 November; Christmas Day, 25 December; Boxing Day, 26 December.

UNITED STATES OF AMERICA
New Year's Day, 1 January; Martin Luther King Day, 18 January; Presidents' Day, 15 February; Memorial Day, 31 May; Independence Day, 4 July; Labour Day, 6 September; Columbus Day, 11 October; Veterans Day, 11 November; Thanksgiving Day, 25 November; Christmas Day, 25 December.

CANADA
New Year's Day, 1 January; Family Day, 15 February; Heritage Day, 15 February; Commonwealth Day, 8 March; St Patrick's Day, 17 March; Good Friday, 2 April; Easter Monday, 5 April; Victoria Day 24 May; Canada Day, 1 July; Labour Day, 6 September; Thanksgiving Day, 11 October; Rememberance Day, 11 November; Christmas Day, 25 December; Boxing Day, 26 December.

AUSTRALIA (NATIONAL HOLIDAYS)
New Year's Day, 1 January; Australia Day, 26 January; Good Friday, 2 April; Easter Monday, 5 April; Anzac Day 25 April; Queen's Birthday, 14 June; Christmas Day, 25 December; Boxing Day, 26 December.

CONTACTS

Name:
Tel:
Email:
Notes:

Name:
Tel:
Email:
Notes:

Name:
Tel:
Email:
Notes:

Name:
Tel:
Email:
Notes:

Name:
Tel:
Email:
Notes:

Name:
Tel:
Email:
Notes:

Name:
Tel:
Email:
Notes:

Name:
Tel:
Email:
Notes:

Name:
Tel:
Email:
Notes:

CONTACTS

Name:
Tel:
Email:
Notes:

Name:
Tel:
Email:
Notes:

Name:
Tel:
Email:
Notes:

Name:
Tel:
Email:
Notes:

Name:
Tel:
Email:
Notes:

Name:
Tel:
Email:
Notes:

Name:
Tel:
Email:
Notes:

Name:
Tel:
Email:
Notes:

Name:
Tel:
Email:
Notes:

CONTACTS

Name:
Tel:
Email:
Notes:

Name:
Tel:
Email:
Notes:

Name:
Tel:
Email:
Notes:

Name:
Tel:
Email:
Notes:

Name:
Tel:
Email:
Notes:

Name:
Tel:
Email:
Notes:

Name:
Tel:
Email:
Notes:

Name:
Tel:
Email:
Notes:

Name:
Tel:
Email:
Notes:

ASPIRATIONS, INTENTIONS AND PROMISES

Follow your Dream

START THE YEAR WITH A PROMISE TO YOURSELF.

This year, I promise:

This year, my dream is:

This year, I intend:

This year, my focus is:

MY BIG WHY

These are the reasons why I deserve success and happiness this year:

This time next year, I will be:

Signed:

JANUARY

Art washes away from the soul the dust of every day life.

Picasso

JANUARY AT A GLANCE

MONDAY	TUESDAY	WEDNESDAY	THURSDAY	FRIDAY	SATURDAY	SUNDAY
				1	2	3
4	5	6	7	8	9	10
11	12	13	14	15	16	17
18	19	20	21	22	23	24
25	26	27	28	29	30	31

A goal is a dream with a deadline

Dates/days to celebrate:

Events to attend:

People to meet/follow up:

Appointments to keep:

Trips to plan:

Purchases/payments to make:

Friends/family to contact:

Movies to see/books to read:

JANUARY

Monthly motivator

PRIORITIES

GOALS

CHALLENGES

ACTIONS

JANUARY

Wheel of life

MY SATISFACTION RATING

Indicate your % on the circle:
Give yourself a score between 0% and 100% on each section now and again at the end of the year on page 456. See your progress and satisfaction rating

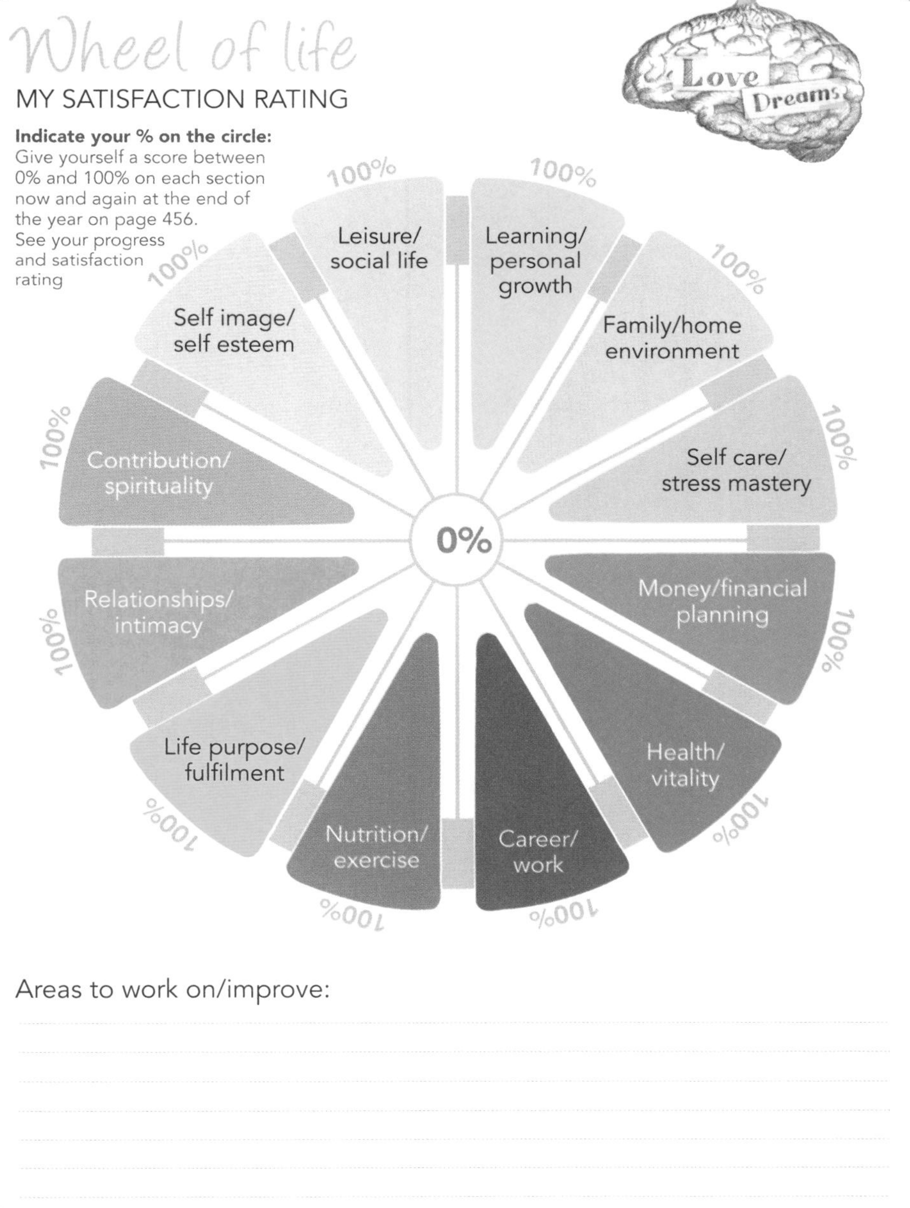

Areas to work on/improve:

JANUARY

5 TIPS OF TIME MANAGEMENT

- Create a daily list of tasks.
- Give each task a priority – 'A, B, C'.
- Work on 'A' tasks first.
- Set a timeline for start and finish .
- Avoid excuses – do it now!

JANUARY

Financial tracker

MONTHLY CASH FLOW

	Personal	Business	Total
Income			
Salary			
Business dividend			
Pension			
Subsidy			
Other			
Total			
Living expenses			
Mortgage/rent			
Utilities/bills			
Credit card payments			
Loan repayments			
Insurance (home/car/life/health)			
Tax (personal/car/property)			
Savings			
Pension/investments			
House/garden			
Travel/fuel			
Groceries/toiletries			
Entertainment/dining out			
Education/training			
Child care			
Home care			
Health/self care/gym			
Other			
Total			
Total income			
Total outgoings			
Surplus/deficit			
This month's priority			

JANUARY

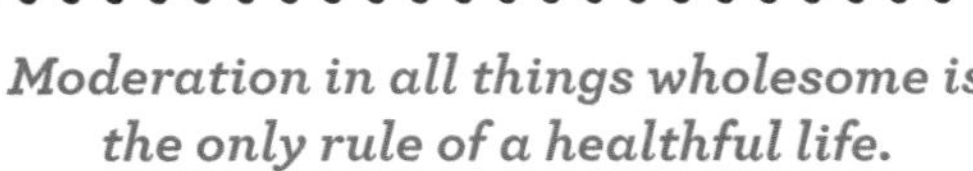

Food planner

Moderation in all things wholesome is the only rule of a healthful life.

MY MENU PLANNER (grocery list)

Week 1

Week 2

Week 3

Week 4

Reflections and comments:

This month's meal ideas:

He who takes medicine and neglects his diet wastes the skill of his doctors.
Chinese proverb

MY HEALTHY NUTRITION PLAN

	BREAKFAST	LUNCH	DINNER	SNACKS	FRUIT	VEGETABLES	WATER
Week 1							
Week 2							
Week 3							
Week 4							

Reflections and comments:

This month's healthy eating ideas:

JANUARY

Health planner

Walking is man's best friend.
Hippocrates

MY EXERCISE PLAN

	ACTIVITY	DURATION	HR	WT/BMI	NOTES
Week 1					
Week 2					
Week 3					
Week 4					

Reflections and comments:

This month's fitness goal:

I choose to be happy because it is good for my health.
Voltaire

MY WELLBEING PLAN

	PHYSICAL	MENTAL/EMOTIONAL	SOCIAL	FINANCIAL
Week 1				
Week 2				
Week 3				
Week 4				

Reflections and comments:

This month's wellbeing goal:

MY IDEAL DAY

EVERY DAY!

MORNING

Morning meditation:

Daily affirmation:

Intention for today:

Ideal breakfast:

Exercise routine:

Getting things done:

Dealing with distractions:

Time for lunch:

AFTERNOON

Getting things done:

Requesting support:

Powerful conversations:

Fun time:

EVENING

Time for dinner:

Me time:

Quality time with significant others:

Getting complete with my day:

Reflection:

Gratitude:

NIGHT

Sleep peacefully

Things to avoid:

Things to include:

Things to notice:

Things to learn:

Things to acknowledge:

Use a pencil and review regularly.

As I began to love myself, I found that anguish and emotional suffering are only warning signs that I was living against my own truth.
Today, I know this is authenticity.

As I began to love myself, I understood how much it can offend somebody if I try to force my desires on this person, even though I knew the time was not right, and the person was not ready for it, and even though this person was me.
Today, I call this respect.

As I began to love myself, I stopped craving for a different life, and I could see that everything that surrounded me was inviting me to grow.
Today, I call this maturity.

As I began to love myself, I understood that at any circumstance, I am in the right place at the right time, and everything happens at the exactly right moment. So I could be calm.
Today, I call this self-confidence.

As I began to love myself, I quit stealing my own time, and I stopped designing huge projects for the future. Today, I only do what brings me joy and happiness, things I love to do and that make my heart cheer, and I do them in my own way and in my own rhythm.
Today I call this simplicity.

As I began to love myself, I freed myself of anything that is no good for my health – food, people, things, situations, and everything that drew me down and away from myself. At first I called this attitude a healthy egoism.
Today, I know it is love of oneself.

As I began to love myself, I quit trying to always be right, and ever since, I was wrong less of the time.
Today, I discovered that is modesty.

As I began to love myself, I refused to go on living in the past and worrying about the future. Now, I only live for the moment, where everything is happening.
Today, I live each day, day by day, and I call it fulfillment.

As I began to love myself, I recognised that my mind can disturb me and it can make me sick. But as I connected it to my heart, my mind became a valuable ally.
Today, I call this connection wisdom of the heart.

We no longer need to fear arguments, confrontations or any kind of problems with ourselves or others. Even stars collide, and out of their crashing, new worlds are born.
Today, I know: this is life!

Charlie Chaplin

JANUARY • New Year's Day

FRIDAY 1

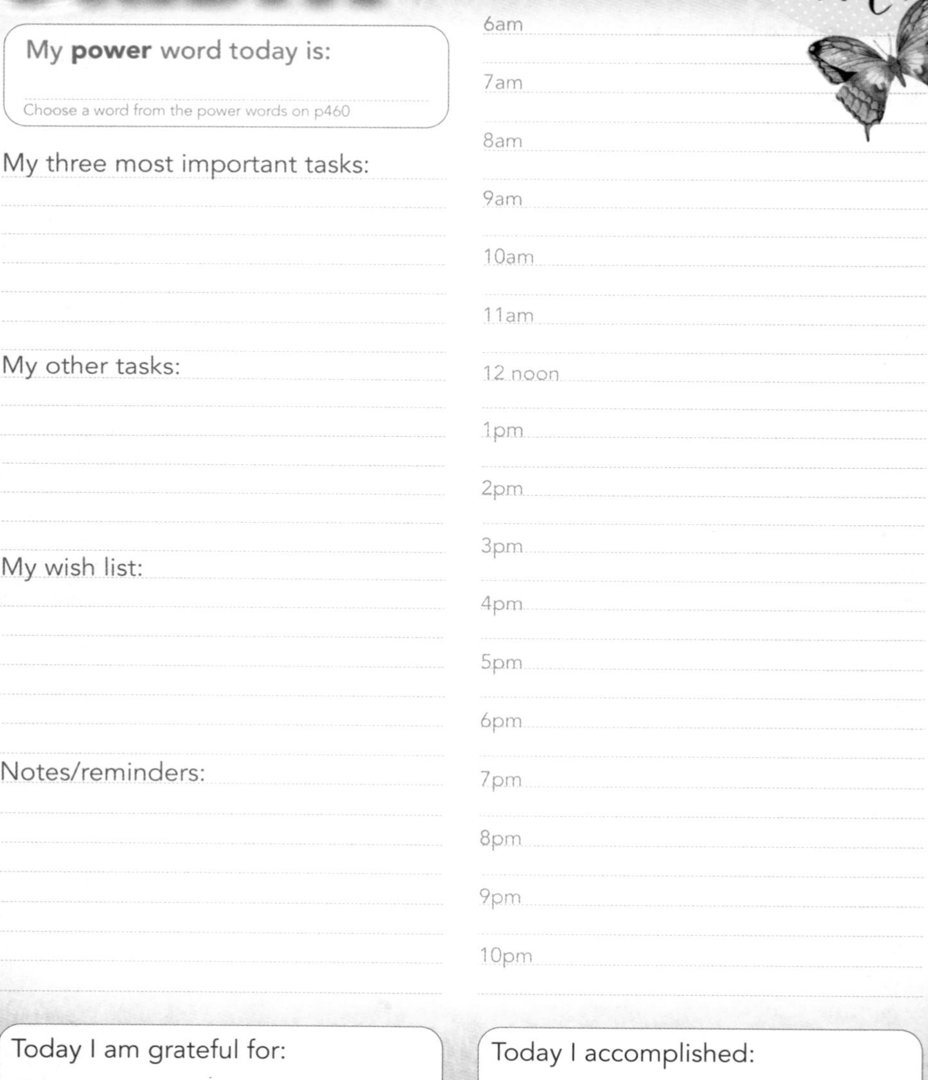

My **power** word today is:

Choose a word from the power words on p460

My three most important tasks:

My other tasks:

My wish list:

Notes/reminders:

6am

7am

8am

9am

10am

11am

12 noon

1pm

2pm

3pm

4pm

5pm

6pm

7pm

8pm

9pm

10pm

Today I am grateful for:

Today I accomplished:

Ask the universe for advice.

SATURDAY 2

My **power** word today is:

Choose a word from the power words on p460

SUNDAY 3

My **power** word today is:

Choose a word from the power words on p460

Every problem has a solution.

JANUARY

MONDAY 4

This week's focus:

My **power** word today is:

Choose a word from the power words on p460

My three most important tasks:

My other tasks:

My wish list:

Notes/reminders:

6am

7am

8am

9am

10am

11am

12 noon

1pm

2pm

3pm

4pm

5pm

6pm

7pm

8pm

9pm

10pm

Today I am grateful for:

Today I accomplished:

All you give is given to yourself.

JANUARY

TUESDAY 5

My **power** word today is:

Choose a word from the power words on p460

My three most important tasks:

My other tasks:

My wish list:

Notes/reminders:

6am

7am

8am

9am

10am

11am

12 noon

1pm

2pm

3pm

4pm

5pm

6pm

7pm

8pm

9pm

10pm

Today I am grateful for:

Today I accomplished:

Don't let yesterday's failures sabotage todays efforts.

JANUARY

WEDNESDAY 6

My **power** word today is:

Choose a word from the power words on p460

My three most important tasks:

My other tasks:

My wish list:

Notes/reminders:

6am

7am

8am

9am

10am

11am

12 noon

1pm

2pm

3pm

4pm

5pm

6pm

7pm

8pm

9pm

10pm

Today I am grateful for:

Today I accomplished:

The world stands aside for the person who knows where she is going.

JANUARY

THURSDAY 7

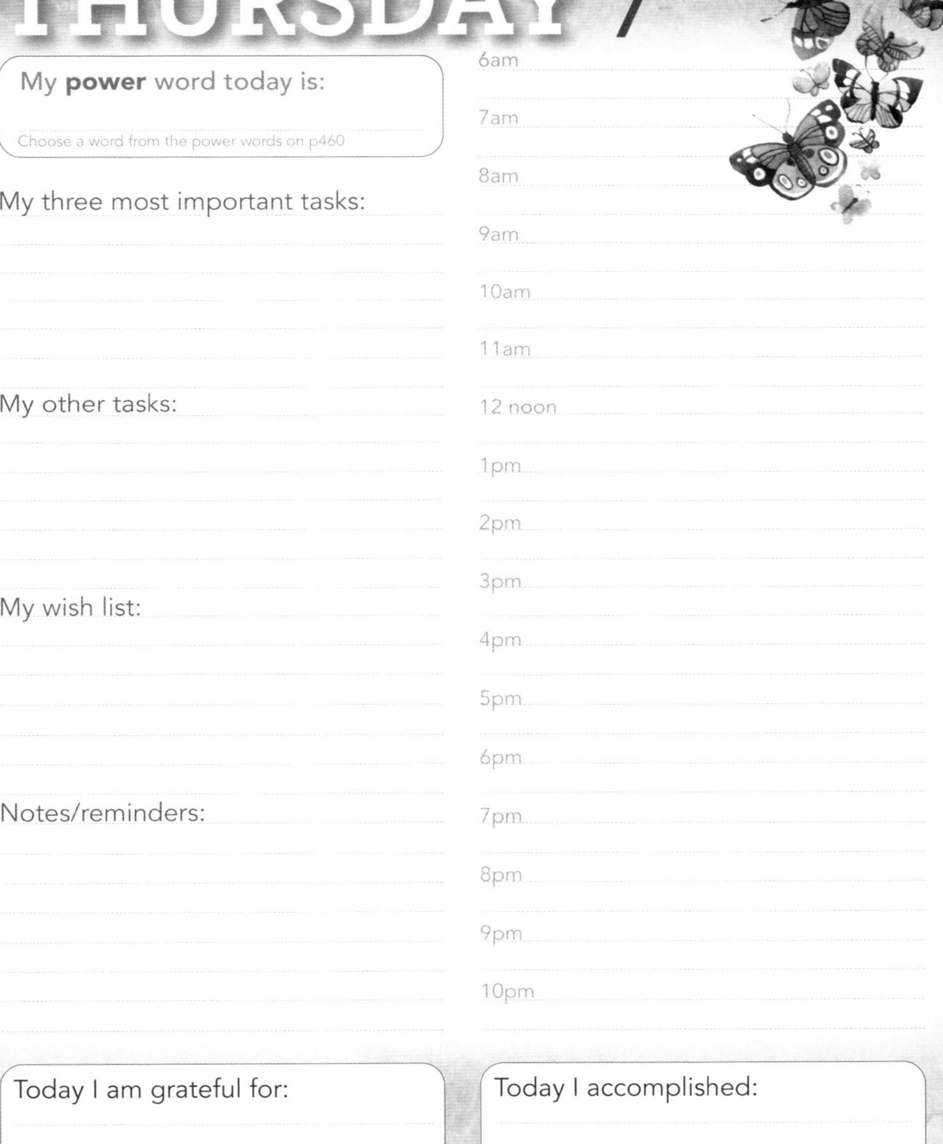

My **power** word today is:

Choose a word from the power words on p460

My three most important tasks:

My other tasks:

My wish list:

Notes/reminders:

6am

7am

8am

9am

10am

11am

12 noon

1pm

2pm

3pm

4pm

5pm

6pm

7pm

8pm

9pm

10pm

Today I am grateful for:

Today I accomplished:

The written word is a crystallised thought.

JANUARY

FRIDAY 8

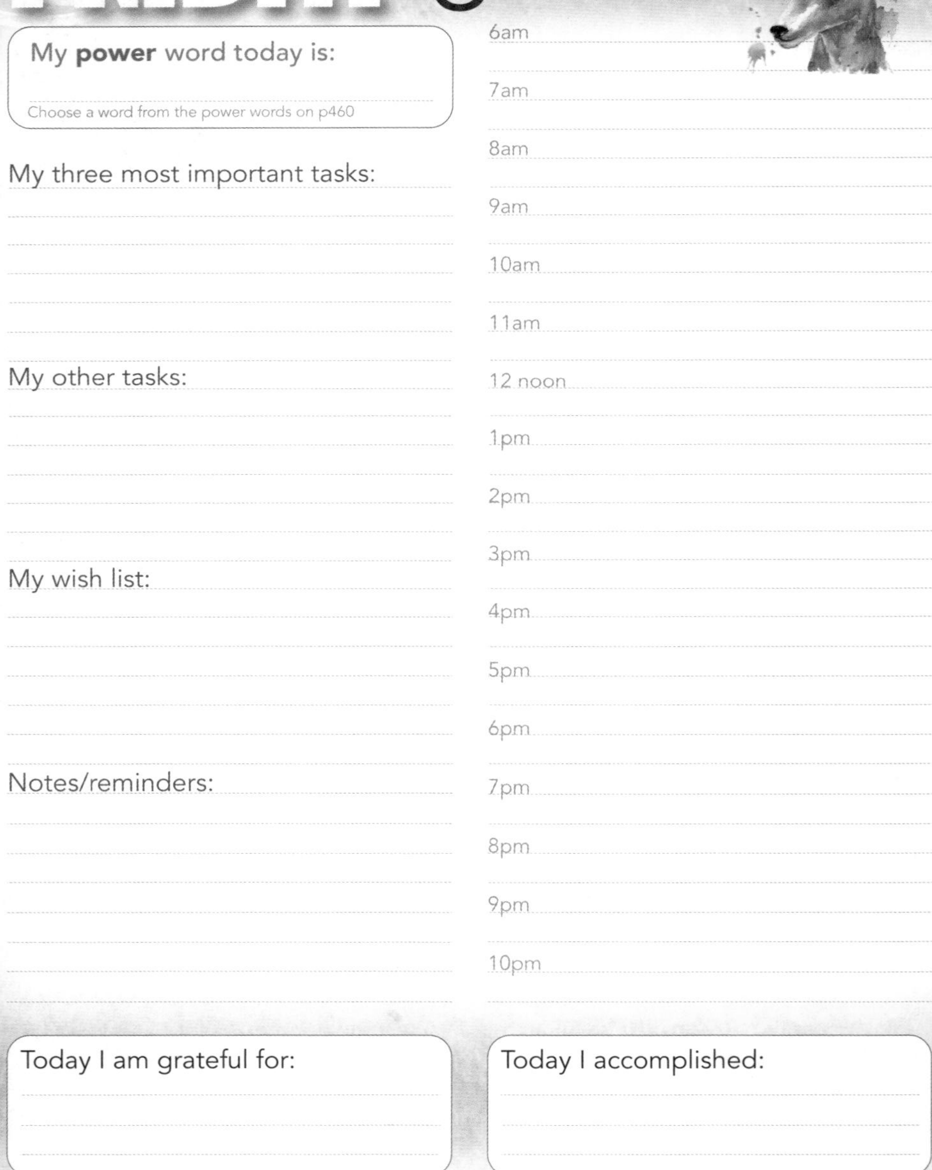

My **power** word today is:

Choose a word from the power words on p460

My three most important tasks:

My other tasks:

My wish list:

Notes/reminders:

6am

7am

8am

9am

10am

11am

12 noon

1pm

2pm

3pm

4pm

5pm

6pm

7pm

8pm

9pm

10pm

Today I am grateful for:

Today I accomplished:

Genius is 99% perspiration, 1% inspiration.

SATURDAY 9

My **power** word today is:

Choose a word from the power words on p460

SUNDAY 10

My **power** word today is:

Choose a word from the power words on p460

If in doubt, honour your word.

JANUARY

MONDAY 11

This week's focus:

My **power** word today is:

Choose a word from the power words on p460

My three most important tasks:

My other tasks:

My wish list:

Notes/reminders:

6am

7am

8am

9am

10am

11am

12 noon

1pm

2pm

3pm

4pm

5pm

6pm

7pm

8pm

9pm

10pm

Today I am grateful for:

Today I accomplished:

Do not get discouraged.

TUESDAY 12

My **power** word today is:

Choose a word from the power words on p460

My three most important tasks:

My other tasks:

My wish list:

Notes/reminders:

6am

7am

8am

9am

10am

11am

12 noon

1pm

2pm

3pm

4pm

5pm

6pm

7pm

8pm

9pm

10pm

Today I am grateful for:

Today I accomplished:

Treat obstacles as challenges.

JANUARY

WEDNESDAY 13

My **power** word today is:

Choose a word from the power words on p460

My three most important tasks:

My other tasks:

My wish list:

Notes/reminders:

6am

7am

8am

9am

10am

11am

12 noon

1pm

2pm

3pm

4pm

5pm

6pm

7pm

8pm

9pm

10pm

Today I am grateful for:

Today I accomplished:

It's what you do right now that matters.

JANUARY

THURSDAY 14

My **power** word today is:

Choose a word from the power words on p460

My three most important tasks:

My other tasks:

My wish list:

Notes/reminders:

6am

7am

8am

9am

10am

11am

12 noon

1pm

2pm

3pm

4pm

5pm

6pm

7pm

8pm

9pm

10pm

Today I am grateful for:

Today I accomplished:

Where there's a will, there's a way.

JANUARY

FRIDAY 15

My **power** word today is:

Choose a word from the power words on p460

My three most important tasks:

My other tasks:

My wish list:

Notes/reminders:

6am

7am

8am

9am

10am

11am

12 noon

1pm

2pm

3pm

4pm

5pm

6pm

7pm

8pm

9pm

10pm

Today I am grateful for:

Today I accomplished:

Trust your intuition.

SATURDAY 16

My **power** word today is:

Choose a word from the power words on p460

SUNDAY 17

My **power** word today is:

Choose a word from the power words on p460

Miracles are happening everywhere.

JANUARY

MONDAY 18

This week's focus:

My **power** word today is:

Choose a word from the power words on p460

6am

7am

8am

9am

10am

11am

12 noon

1pm

2pm

3pm

4pm

5pm

6pm

7pm

8pm

9pm

10pm

My three most important tasks:

My other tasks:

My wish list:

Notes/reminders:

Today I am grateful for:

Today I accomplished:

Speak and act with a kind heart.

JANUARY

TUESDAY 19

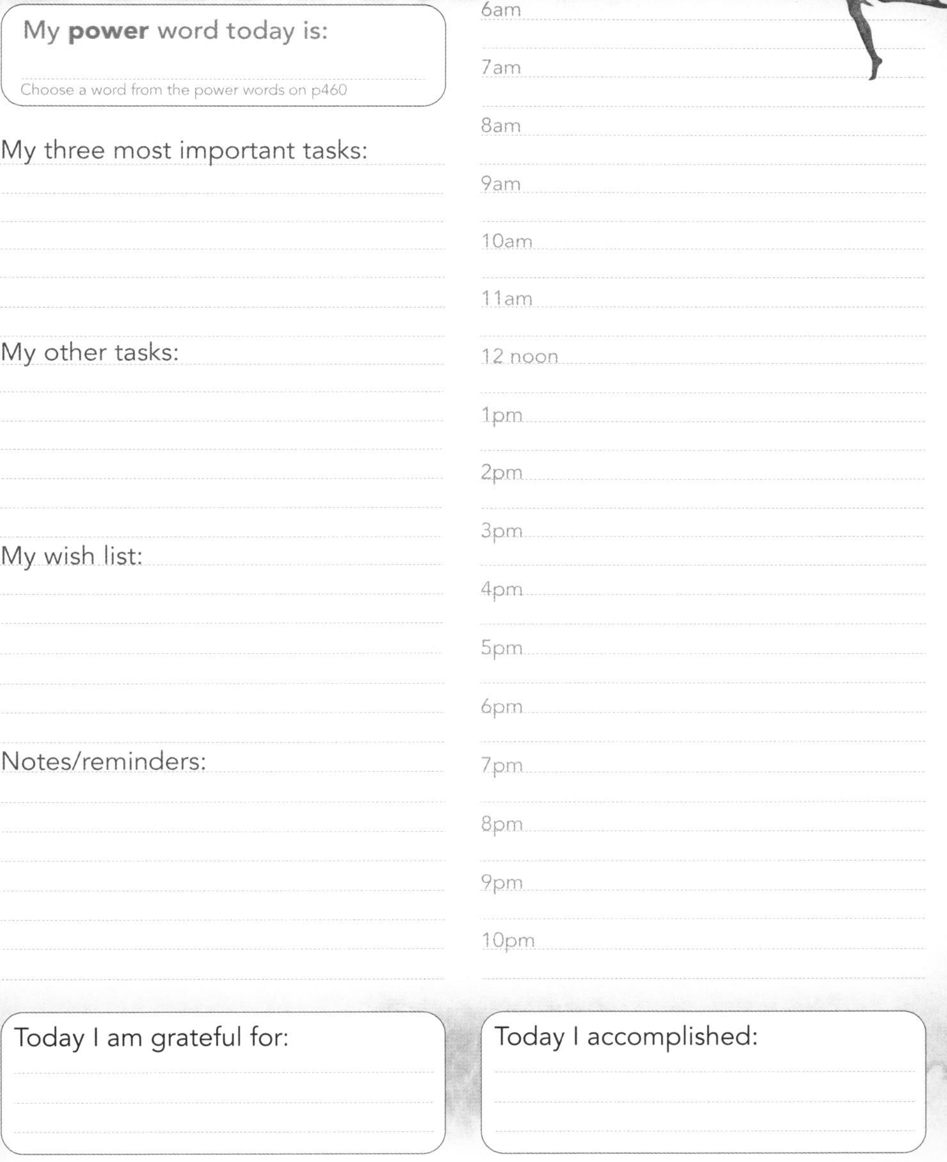

My **power** word today is:

Choose a word from the power words on p460

My three most important tasks:

My other tasks:

My wish list:

Notes/reminders:

6am

7am

8am

9am

10am

11am

12 noon

1pm

2pm

3pm

4pm

5pm

6pm

7pm

8pm

9pm

10pm

Today I am grateful for:

Today I accomplished:

The truth is not always easy to hear, or speak.

JANUARY

WEDNESDAY 20

My **power** word today is:

Choose a word from the power words on p460

My three most important tasks:

My other tasks:

My wish list:

Notes/reminders:

6am

7am

8am

9am

10am

11am

12 noon

1pm

2pm

3pm

4pm

5pm

6pm

7pm

8pm

9pm

10pm

Today I am grateful for:

Today I accomplished:

As you start to walk, the way appears.

JANUARY

THURSDAY 21

My **power** word today is:

Choose a word from the power words on p460

My three most important tasks:

My other tasks:

My wish list:

Notes/reminders:

6am

7am

8am

9am

10am

11am

12 noon

1pm

2pm

3pm

4pm

5pm

6pm

7pm

8pm

9pm

10pm

Today I am grateful for:

Today I accomplished:

Get excited about what might go right.

JANUARY

FRIDAY 22

My **power** word today is:

Choose a word from the power words on p460

My three most important tasks:

My other tasks:

My wish list:

Notes/reminders:

6am

7am

8am

9am

10am

11am

12 noon

1pm

2pm

3pm

4pm

5pm

6pm

7pm

8pm

9pm

10pm

Today I am grateful for:

Today I accomplished:

Be honest about how you really feel.

SATURDAY 23

My **power** word today is:

Choose a word from the power words on p460

SUNDAY 24

My **power** word today is:

Choose a word from the power words on p460

Luck is where preparation meets opportunity.

JANUARY

MONDAY 25

This week's focus:

My **power** word today is:

Choose a word from the power words on p460

My three most important tasks:

My other tasks:

My wish list:

Notes/reminders:

6am

7am

8am

9am

10am

11am

12 noon

1pm

2pm

3pm

4pm

5pm

6pm

7pm

8pm

9pm

10pm

Today I am grateful for:

Today I accomplished:

Well done is better than well said.

JANUARY

TUESDAY 26

My **power** word today is:

Choose a word from the power words on p460

My three most important tasks:

My other tasks:

My wish list:

Notes/reminders:

6am

7am

8am

9am

10am

11am

12 noon

1pm

2pm

3pm

4pm

5pm

6pm

7pm

8pm

9pm

10pm

Today I am grateful for:

Today I accomplished:

Every accomplishment starts with a decision to try.

JANUARY

WEDNESDAY 27

My **power** word today is:

Choose a word from the power words on p460

My three most important tasks:

My other tasks:

My wish list:

Notes/reminders:

6am

7am

8am

9am

10am

11am

12 noon

1pm

2pm

3pm

4pm

5pm

6pm

7pm

8pm

9pm

10pm

Today I am grateful for:

Today I accomplished:

When you're tempted, remember what you promised.

JANUARY

THURSDAY 28

My **power** word today is:

Choose a word from the power words on p460

My three most important tasks:

My other tasks:

My wish list:

Notes/reminders:

6am

7am

8am

9am

10am

11am

12 noon

1pm

2pm

3pm

4pm

5pm

6pm

7pm

8pm

9pm

10pm

Today I am grateful for:

Today I accomplished:

Every day is a new opportunity to start over.

JANUARY

FRIDAY 29

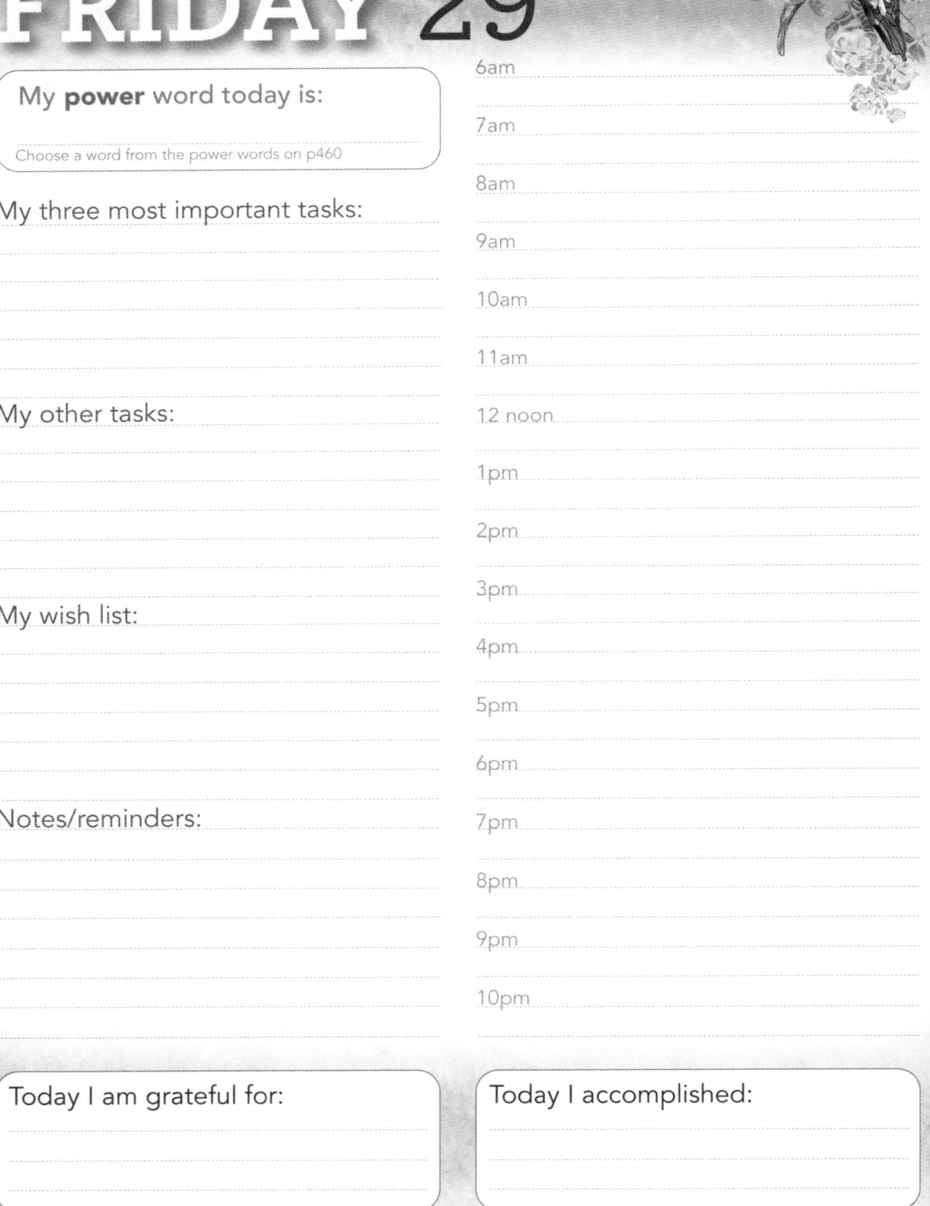

My **power** word today is:

Choose a word from the power words on p460

My three most important tasks:

My other tasks:

My wish list:

Notes/reminders:

6am

7am

8am

9am

10am

11am

12 noon

1pm

2pm

3pm

4pm

5pm

6pm

7pm

8pm

9pm

10pm

Today I am grateful for:

Today I accomplished:

No matter how you feel, get up, dress up and show up.

SATURDAY 30

My **power** word today is:

Choose a word from the power words on p460

SUNDAY 31

My **power** word today is:

Choose a word from the power words on p460

Plan your work and work your plan.

THE INVITATION

It doesn't interest me what you do for a living. I want to know what you ache for, and if you dare to dream of meeting your heart's longing. It doesn't interest me how old you are. I want to know if you will risk looking like a fool for love, for your dream, for the adventure of being alive.

It doesn't interest me what planets are squaring your moon. I want to know if you have touched the centre of your own sorrow, if you have been opened by life's betrayals or have become shrivelled and closed from fear of further pain! I want to know if you can sit with pain, mine or your own, without moving to hide it or fade it, or fix it.

I want to know if you can be with joy, mine or your own, if you can dance with wildness and let the ecstasy fill you to the tips of your fingers and toes without cautioning us to be careful, to be realistic, to remember the limitations of being human. It doesn't interest me if the story you are telling me is true. I want to know if you can disappoint another to be true to yourself; if you can bear the accusation of betrayal and not betray your own soul; if you can be faithless and therefore trustworthy.

I want to know if you can see beauty even when it's not pretty, every day, and if you can source your own life from its presence. I want to know if you can live with failure, yours and mine, and still stand on the edge of the lake and shout to the silver of the full moon, "Yes!" It doesn't interest me to know where you live or how much money you have. I want to know if you can get up, after the night of grief and despair, weary and bruised to the bone, and do what needs to be done to feed the children.

It doesn't interest me who you know or how you came to be here. I want to know if you will stand in the centre of the fire with me and not shrink back. It doesn't interest me where or what or with whom you have studied. I want to know what sustains you, from the inside, when all else falls away. I want to know if you can be alone with yourself and if you truly like the company you keep in the empty moments.

Oriah Mountain Dreamer

JANUARY

Monthly reflections

You see things; and you say, 'Why?' But I dream things that never were; and I say, 'Why not?'
George Bernard Shaw

Best moments:

Greatest accomplishments:

Toughest challenge:

Biggest learnings:

Progress towards ongoing goals:

Remember your 2021 promises and your BIG WHY.
Remind yourself of your motives on page 10.

WHY NOT YOU?

I request THE Highest OF FIVES

Today, many will awaken with a fresh sense of inspiration. Why not you?

Today, many will open their eyes to the beauty that surrounds them. Why not you?

Today, many will choose to leave the ghost of yesterday behind and seize the immeasurable power of today. Why not you?

Today, many will break through the barriers of the past by looking at the blessings of the present. Why not you?

Today, for many the burden of self doubt and insecurity will be lifted by the security and confidence of empowerment. Why not you?

Today, many will rise above their believed limitations and make contact with their powerful innate strength. Why not you?

Today, many will choose to live in such a manner that they will be a positive role model for their children. Why not you?

Today, many will choose to free themselves from the personal imprisonment of their bad habits. Why not you?

Today, many will choose to live free of conditions and rules governing their own happiness. Why not you?

Today, many will find abundance in simplicity. Why not you?

Today, many will be confronted by difficult moral choices and they will choose to do what is right instead of what is beneficial. Why not you?

Today, many will decide to no longer sit back with a victim mentality, but to take charge of their lives and make positive changes. Why not you?

Today, many will take the action necessary to make a difference. Why not you?

Today, many will make the commitment to be a better mother, father, son, daughter, student, teacher, worker, boss, brother, sister, and so much more. Why not you?

Today is a new day!
Many will seize this day.
Many will live it to the fullest.
Why not you?

Steve Maraboli

FEBRUARY

The most powerful weapon on earth is the human soul on fire.

Ferdinand Foch

FEBRUARY AT A GLANCE

MONDAY	TUESDAY	WEDNESDAY	THURSDAY	FRIDAY	SATURDAY	SUNDAY
1	2	3	4	5	6	7
8	9	10	11	12	13	14
15	16	17	18	19	20	21
22	23	24	25	26	27	28

FEBRUARY ACTION PLANNER

A goal is a dream with a deadline

Dates/days to celebrate:

Events to attend:

People to meet/follow up:

Appointments to keep:

Trips to plan:

Purchases/payments to make:

Friends/family to contact:

Movies to see/books to read:

FEBRUARY

Monthly motivator

PRIORITIES

GOALS

CHALLENGES

ACTIONS

FEBRUARY

Financial tracker

MONTHLY CASH FLOW

	Personal	Business	Total
Income			
Salary			
Business dividend			
Pension			
Subsidy			
Other			
Total			
Living expenses			
Mortgage/rent			
Utilities/bills			
Credit card payments			
Loan repayments			
Insurance (home/car/life/health)			
Tax (personal/car/property)			
Savings			
Pension/investments			
House/garden			
Travel/fuel			
Groceries/toiletries			
Entertainment/dining out			
Education/training			
Child care			
Home care			
Health/self care/gym			
Other			
Total			
Total income			
Total outgoings			
Surplus/deficit			
This month's priority			

FEBRUARY

Food planner

Garbage in, garbage out.
George Fuechsel

MY MENU PLANNER (grocery list)

Week 1

Week 2

Week 3

Week 4

Reflections and comments:

This month's meal ideas:

Let food be thy medicine and medicine be thy food.
Hippocrates

MY HEALTHY NUTRITION PLAN

	BREAKFAST	LUNCH	DINNER	SNACKS	FRUIT	VEGETABLES	WATER
Week 1							
Week 2							
Week 3							
Week 4							

Reflections and comments:

This month's healthy eating ideas:

FEBRUARY

Health planner

The greatest wealth is health.
Virgil

MY EXERCISE PLAN

	ACTIVITY	DURATION	HR	WT/BMI	NOTES
Week 1					
Week 2					
Week 3					
Week 4					

Reflections and comments:

This month's fitness goal:

When the heart is at ease, the body is healthy.
Chinese proverb

MY WELLBEING PLAN

	PHYSICAL	MENTAL/EMOTIONAL	SOCIAL	FINANCIAL
Week 1				
Week 2				
Week 3				
Week 4				

Reflections and comments:

This month's wellbeing goal:

FEBRUARY

Doodles and ideas

5 TIPS TO WELLBEING

- Stay positive.
- Ask for what you need.
- Let people support you.
- Do what you enjoy.
- Avoid negative influences.

FEBRUARY

MONDAY 1

This week's focus:

My **power** word today is:

Choose a word from the power words on p460

My three most important tasks:

My other tasks:

My wish list:

Notes/reminders:

6am

7am

8am

9am

10am

11am

12 noon

1pm

2pm

3pm

4pm

5pm

6pm

7pm

8pm

9pm

10pm

Today I am grateful for:

Today I accomplished:

Appreciate the lesson you are being taught.

FEBRUARY

TUESDAY 2

My **power** word today is:

Choose a word from the power words on p460

My three most important tasks:

My other tasks:

My wish list:

Notes/reminders:

6am

7am

8am

9am

10am

11am

12 noon

1pm

2pm

3pm

4pm

5pm

6pm

7pm

8pm

9pm

10pm

Today I am grateful for:

Today I accomplished:

Make big promises and grow into them.

FEBRUARY

WEDNESDAY 3

My **power** word today is:

Choose a word from the power words on p460

My three most important tasks:

My other tasks:

My wish list:

Notes/reminders:

6am

7am

8am

9am

10am

11am

12 noon

1pm

2pm

3pm

4pm

5pm

6pm

7pm

8pm

9pm

10pm

Today I am grateful for:

Today I accomplished:

Value your friends for who they are.

FEBRUARY

THURSDAY 4

My **power** word today is:

Choose a word from the power words on p460

My three most important tasks:

My other tasks:

My wish list:

Notes/reminders:

6am

7am

8am

9am

10am

11am

12 noon

1pm

2pm

3pm

4pm

5pm

6pm

7pm

8pm

9pm

10pm

Today I am grateful for:

Today I accomplished:

Do not gossip.

FEBRUARY

FRIDAY 5

My **power** word today is:

Choose a word from the power words on p460

My three most important tasks:

My other tasks:

My wish list:

Notes/reminders:

6am

7am

8am

9am

10am

11am

12 noon

1pm

2pm

3pm

4pm

5pm

6pm

7pm

8pm

9pm

10pm

Today I am grateful for:

Today I accomplished:

Write down your ideas.

SATURDAY 6

My **power** word today is:

Choose a word from the power words on p460

SUNDAY 7

My **power** word today is:

Choose a word from the power words on p460

Be confident in your abilities.

FEBRUARY

MONDAY 8

This week's focus:

My **power** word today is:

Choose a word from the power words on p460

My three most important tasks:

My other tasks:

My wish list:

Notes/reminders:

6am

7am

8am

9am

10am

11am

12 noon

1pm

2pm

3pm

4pm

5pm

6pm

7pm

8pm

9pm

10pm

Today I am grateful for:

Today I accomplished:

Practice makes perfect.

FEBRUARY

TUESDAY 9

My **power** word today is:

Choose a word from the power words on p460

My three most important tasks:

My other tasks:

My wish list:

Notes/reminders:

6am

7am

8am

9am

10am

11am

12 noon

1pm

2pm

3pm

4pm

5pm

6pm

7pm

8pm

9pm

10pm

Today I am grateful for:

Today I accomplished:

Go for a walk to clear your head.

FEBRUARY

WEDNESDAY 10

My **power** word today is:

Choose a word from the power words on p460

My three most important tasks:

My other tasks:

My wish list:

Notes/reminders:

6am

7am

8am

9am

10am

11am

12 noon

1pm

2pm

3pm

4pm

5pm

6pm

7pm

8pm

9pm

10pm

Today I am grateful for:

Today I accomplished:

Stop judging yourself.

FEBRUARY

THURSDAY 11

My **power** word today is:

Choose a word from the power words on p460

My three most important tasks:

My other tasks:

My wish list:

Notes/reminders:

6am

7am

8am

9am

10am

11am

12 noon

1pm

2pm

3pm

4pm

5pm

6pm

7pm

8pm

9pm

10pm

Today I am grateful for:

Today I accomplished:

Say something to brighten another's day.

FEBRUARY

FRIDAY 12

My **power** word today is:

Choose a word from the power words on p460

My three most important tasks:

My other tasks:

My wish list:

Notes/reminders:

6am

7am

8am

9am

10am

11am

12 noon

1pm

2pm

3pm

4pm

5pm

6pm

7pm

8pm

9pm

10pm

Today I am grateful for:

Today I accomplished:

Read more books.

SATURDAY 13

My **power** word today is:

Choose a word from the power words on p460

SUNDAY 14 St Valentine's Day

My **power** word today is:

Choose a word from the power words on p460

Listen to your heart

Smile at the person in the mirror.

FEBRUARY

MONDAY 15

This week's focus:

My **power** word today is:

Choose a word from the power words on p460

6am

7am

8am

9am

10am

11am

12 noon

1pm

2pm

3pm

4pm

5pm

6pm

7pm

8pm

9pm

10pm

My three most important tasks:

My other tasks:

My wish list:

Notes/reminders:

Today I am grateful for:

Today I accomplished:

Take responsibility for your mistakes.

FEBRUARY

TUESDAY 16

My **power** word today is:

Choose a word from the power words on p460

My three most important tasks:

My other tasks:

My wish list:

Notes/reminders:

6am

7am

8am

9am

10am

11am

12 noon

1pm

2pm

3pm

4pm

5pm

6pm

7pm

8pm

9pm

10pm

Today I am grateful for:

Today I accomplished:

Finish what you start.

FEBRUARY

WEDNESDAY 17

My **power** word today is:

Choose a word from the power words on p460

My three most important tasks:

My other tasks:

My wish list:

Notes/reminders:

6am

7am

8am

9am

10am

11am

12 noon

1pm

2pm

3pm

4pm

5pm

6pm

7pm

8pm

9pm

10pm

Today I am grateful for:

Today I accomplished:

Seek advice and take it.

FEBRUARY

THURSDAY 18

My **power** word today is:

Choose a word from the power words on p460

My three most important tasks:

My other tasks:

My wish list:

Notes/reminders:

6am

7am

8am

9am

10am

11am

12 noon

1pm

2pm

3pm

4pm

5pm

6pm

7pm

8pm

9pm

10pm

Today I am grateful for:

Today I accomplished:

Use everything as an opportunity to learn.

FEBRUARY

FRIDAY 19

My **power** word today is:

Choose a word from the power words on p460

My three most important tasks:

My other tasks:

My wish list:

Notes/reminders:

6am

7am

8am

9am

10am

11am

12 noon

1pm

2pm

3pm

4pm

5pm

6pm

7pm

8pm

9pm

10pm

Today I am grateful for:

Today I accomplished:

Develop a habit of saving for what you want.

SATURDAY 20

My **power** word today is:

Choose a word from the power words on p460

SUNDAY 21

My **power** word today is:

Choose a word from the power words on p460

Don't hope for the best, plan for the best.

FEBRUARY

MONDAY 22

This week's focus:

My **power** word today is:

Choose a word from the power words on p460

My three most important tasks:

My other tasks:

My wish list:

Notes/reminders:

6am

7am

8am

9am

10am

11am

12 noon

1pm

2pm

3pm

4pm

5pm

6pm

7pm

8pm

9pm

10pm

Today I am grateful for:

Today I accomplished:

It will go the way you say.

FEBRUARY

TUESDAY 23

My **power** word today is:

Choose a word from the power words on p460

My three most important tasks:

My other tasks:

My wish list:

Notes/reminders:

6am

7am

8am

9am

10am

11am

12 noon

1pm

2pm

3pm

4pm

5pm

6pm

7pm

8pm

9pm

10pm

Today I am grateful for:

Today I accomplished:

Be willing to make the first move.

FEBRUARY

WEDNESDAY 24

My **power** word today is:

Choose a word from the power words on p460

My three most important tasks:

My other tasks:

My wish list:

Notes/reminders:

6am

7am

8am

9am

10am

11am

12 noon

1pm

2pm

3pm

4pm

5pm

6pm

7pm

8pm

9pm

10pm

Today I am grateful for:

Today I accomplished:

Listen for contribution.

FEBRUARY

THURSDAY 25

My **power** word today is:

Choose a word from the power words on p460

My three most important tasks:

My other tasks:

My wish list:

Notes/reminders:

6am

7am

8am

9am

10am

11am

12 noon

1pm

2pm

3pm

4pm

5pm

6pm

7pm

8pm

9pm

10pm

Today I am grateful for:

Today I accomplished:

Walk your talk.

FEBRUARY

FRIDAY 26

My **power** word today is:

Choose a word from the power words on p460

My three most important tasks:

My other tasks:

My wish list:

Notes/reminders:

6am

7am

8am

9am

10am

11am

12 noon

1pm

2pm

3pm

4pm

5pm

6pm

7pm

8pm

9pm

10pm

Today I am grateful for:

Today I accomplished:

If you mess up, fess up.

SATURDAY 27

My **power** word today is:

Choose a word from the power words on p460

SUNDAY 28

My **power** word today is:

Choose a word from the power words on p460

The truth will set you free.

FEBRUARY

What is not started today is never finished tomorrow.
Johann Wolfgang von Goethe

Best moments:

Greatest accomplishments:

Toughest challenge:

Biggest learnings:

Progress towards ongoing goals:

Remember your 2021 promises and your BIG WHY.
Remind yourself of your motives on page 10.

MARCH

Doodles and ideas

SCRIBBLE

5 TIPS FOR HAPPINESS

- Accept what is
- Follow your heart
- Dream big
- Go with the flow
- Appreciate what you have

MARCH

Start by doing what's necessary; then do what's possible, and suddenly you are doing the impossible.

St Francis of Assisi

MARCH AT A GLANCE

MONDAY	TUESDAY	WEDNESDAY	THURSDAY	FRIDAY	SATURDAY	SUNDAY
1	2	3	4	5	6	7
8	9	10	11	12	13	14
15	16	17	18	19	20	21
22	23	24	25	26	27	28
29	30	31				

MARCH ACTION PLANNER

A goal is a dream with a deadline

Dates/days to celebrate:

Events to attend:

People to meet/follow up:

Appointments to keep:

Trips to plan:

Purchases/payments to make:

Friends/family to contact:

Movies to see/books to read:

MARCH

Monthly motivator

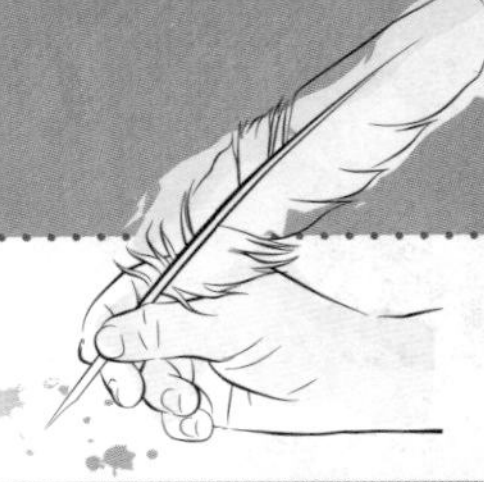

PRIORITIES

GOALS

CHALLENGES

ACTIONS

MARCH

Financial tracker

MONTHLY CASH FLOW

	Personal	Business	Total
Income			
Salary			
Business dividend			
Pension			
Subsidy			
Other			
Total			
Living expenses			
Mortgage/rent			
Utilities/bills			
Credit card payments			
Loan repayments			
Insurance (home/car/life/health)			
Tax (personal/car/property)			
Savings			
Pension/investments			
House/garden			
Travel/fuel			
Groceries/toiletries			
Entertainment/dining out			
Education/training			
Child care			
Home care			
Health/self care/gym			
Other			
Total			
Total income			
Total outgoings			
Surplus/deficit			
This month's priority			

MARCH

Food planner

Eat to live, not live to eat.
Socrates

MY MENU PLANNER (grocery list)

Week 1

Week 2

Week 3

Week 4

Reflections and comments:

This month's meal ideas:

Good health and good sense are two of life's greatest blessings.
Publilius Syrus

MY HEALTHY NUTRITION PLAN

	BREAKFAST	LUNCH	DINNER	SNACKS	FRUIT	VEGETABLES	WATER
Week 1							
Week 2							
Week 3							
Week 4							

Reflections and comments:

This month's healthy eating ideas:

MARCH

Health planner

The groundwork for all happiness is good health.
Leigh Hunt

MY EXERCISE PLAN

	ACTIVITY	DURATION	HR	WT/BMI	NOTES
Week 1					
Week 2					
Week 3					
Week 4					

Reflections and comments:

This month's fitness goal:

If you would live long, open your heart.

MY WELLBEING PLAN

	PHYSICAL	MENTAL/EMOTIONAL	SOCIAL	FINANCIAL
Week 1				
Week 2				
Week 3				
Week 4				

Reflections and comments:

This month's wellbeing goal:

VISION BOARD

Create a vision board for your ideal life.

Working with your 'Future vision' on page 197, write or draw about your ideal life. Then create a visual display using pictures from magazines.

MARCH

MONDAY 1

This week's focus:

My **power** word today is:

Choose a word from the power words on p460

My three most important tasks:

My other tasks:

My wish list:

Notes/reminders:

6am

7am

8am

9am

10am

11am

12 noon

1pm

2pm

3pm

4pm

5pm

6pm

7pm

8pm

9pm

10pm

Today I am grateful for:

Today I accomplished:

Create the future you desire.

MARCH

TUESDAY 2

My power word today is:

Choose a word from the power words on p460

My three most important tasks:

My other tasks:

My wish list:

Notes/reminders:

6am

7am

8am

9am

10am

11am

12 noon

1pm

2pm

3pm

4pm

5pm

6pm

7pm

8pm

9pm

10pm

Today I am grateful for:

Today I accomplished:

Get fit and stay fit.

MARCH

WEDNESDAY 3

My power word today is:

Choose a word from the power words on p460

6am

7am

8am

9am

10am

11am

12 noon

1pm

2pm

3pm

4pm

5pm

6pm

7pm

8pm

9pm

10pm

My three most important tasks:

My other tasks:

My wish list:

Notes/reminders:

Today I am grateful for:

Today I accomplished:

Go with the flow of life.

MARCH

THURSDAY 4

My **power** word today is:

Choose a word from the power words on p460

My three most important tasks:

My other tasks:

My wish list:

Notes/reminders:

6am

7am

8am

9am

10am

11am

12 noon

1pm

2pm

3pm

4pm

5pm

6pm

7pm

8pm

9pm

10pm

Today I am grateful for:

Today I accomplished:

Be generous and fair to everyone.

MARCH

FRIDAY 5

My **power** word today is:

Choose a word from the power words on p460

My three most important tasks:

My other tasks:

My wish list:

Notes/reminders:

6am

7am

8am

9am

10am

11am

12 noon

1pm

2pm

3pm

4pm

5pm

6pm

7pm

8pm

9pm

10pm

Today I am grateful for:

Today I accomplished:

Don't be afraid of criticism.

SATURDAY 6

My **power** word today is:

Choose a word from the power words on p460

SUNDAY 7

My **power** word today is:

Choose a word from the power words on p460

Don't take it personally.

MARCH

MONDAY 8

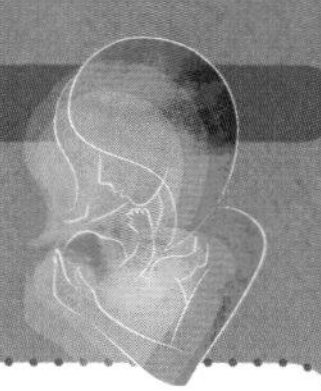

This week's focus:

My power word today is:

Choose a word from the power words on p460

6am

7am

8am

9am

10am

11am

12 noon

1pm

2pm

3pm

4pm

5pm

6pm

7pm

8pm

9pm

10pm

My three most important tasks:

My other tasks:

My wish list:

Notes/reminders:

Today I am grateful for:

Today I accomplished:

Stand back to see the bigger picture.

MARCH

TUESDAY 9

My power word today is:

Choose a word from the power words on p460

My three most important tasks:

My other tasks:

My wish list:

Notes/reminders:

6am

7am

8am

9am

10am

11am

12 noon

1pm

2pm

3pm

4pm

5pm

6pm

7pm

8pm

9pm

10pm

Today I am grateful for:

Today I accomplished:

Do today what you want to put off until tomorrow.

MARCH

WEDNESDAY 10

My power word today is:

Choose a word from the power words on p460

My three most important tasks:

My other tasks:

My wish list:

Notes/reminders:

6am

7am

8am

9am

10am

11am

12 noon

1pm

2pm

3pm

4pm

5pm

6pm

7pm

8pm

9pm

10pm

Today I am grateful for:

Today I accomplished:

Join in and participate.

MARCH

THURSDAY 11

My power word today is:

Choose a word from the power words on p460

My three most important tasks:

My other tasks:

My wish list:

Notes/reminders:

6am

7am

8am

9am

10am

11am

12 noon

1pm

2pm

3pm

4pm

5pm

6pm

7pm

8pm

9pm

10pm

Today I am grateful for:

Today I accomplished:

Acknowledge yourself for your accomplishments.

MARCH

FRIDAY 12

My power word today is:

Choose a word from the power words on p460

on p460

My three most important tasks:

My other tasks:

My wish list:

Notes/reminders:

6am

7am

8am

9am

10am

11am

12 noon

1pm

2pm

3pm

4pm

5pm

6pm

7pm

8pm

9pm

10pm

Today I am grateful for:

Today I accomplished:

Say what needs to be said and accept what comes.

MARCH

SATURDAY 13

My **power** word today is:

Choose a word from the power words on p460

SUNDAY 14 Mothers' Day

My **power** word today is:

Choose a word from the power words on p460

We are free to choose but our choices have consequences.

MARCH

MONDAY 15

This week's focus:

My **power** word today is:

Choose a word from the power words on p460

6am

7am

8am

9am

10am

11am

12 noon

1pm

2pm

3pm

4pm

5pm

6pm

7pm

8pm

9pm

10pm

My three most important tasks:

My other tasks:

My wish list:

Notes/reminders:

Today I am grateful for:

Today I accomplished:

Don't be held back by a bad attitude.

MARCH

TUESDAY 16

My **power** word today is:

Choose a word from the power words on p460

My three most important tasks:

My other tasks:

My wish list:

Notes/reminders:

6am

7am

8am

9am

10am

11am

12 noon

1pm

2pm

3pm

4pm

5pm

6pm

7pm

8pm

9pm

10pm

Today I am grateful for:

Today I accomplished:

Be adaptable to changing circumstances.

MARCH • St Patrick's Day

WEDNESDAY 17

My power word today is:

Choose a word from the power words on p460

My three most important tasks:

My other tasks:

My wish list:

Notes/reminders:

6am

7am

8am

9am

10am

11am

12 noon

1pm

2pm

3pm

4pm

5pm

6pm

7pm

8pm

9pm

10pm

Today I am grateful for:

Today I accomplished:

Failing to prepare is preparing to fail.

MARCH

THURSDAY 18

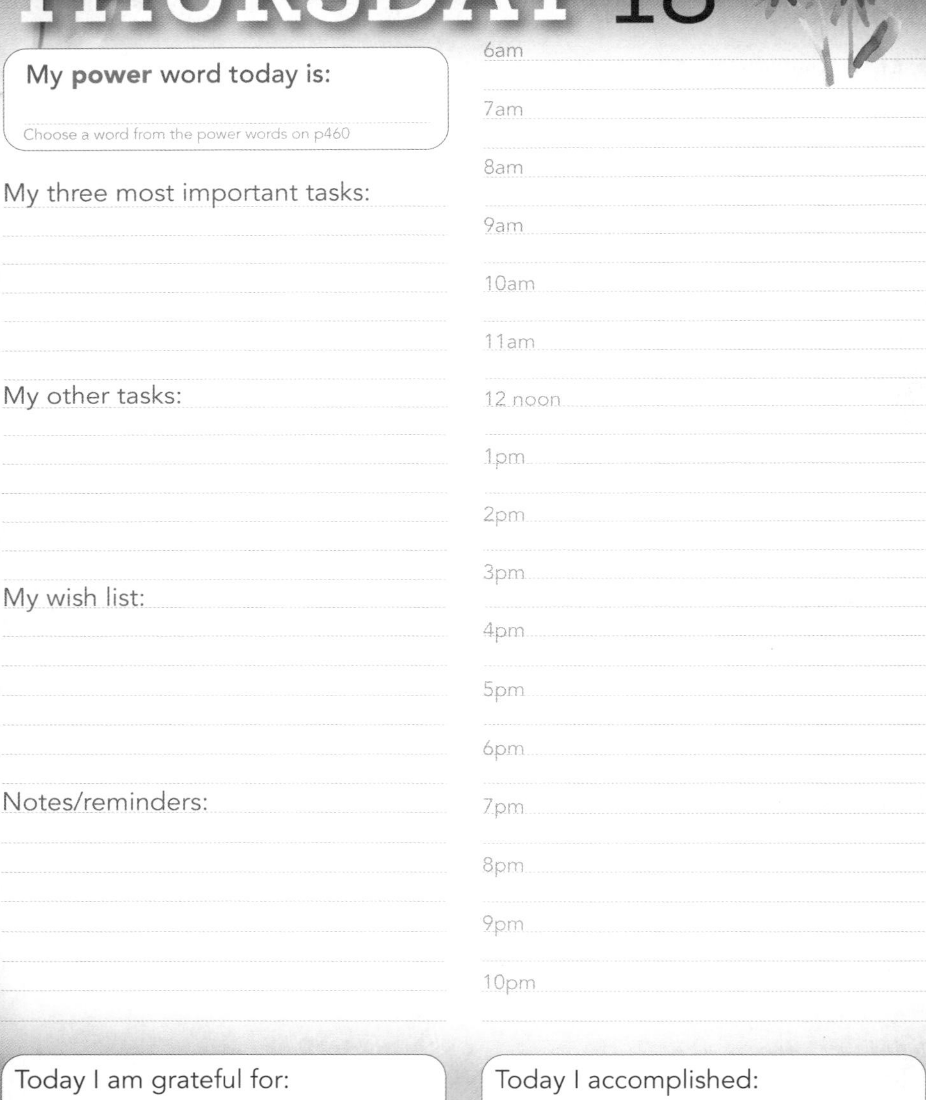

Today I am grateful for:

Today I accomplished:

A problem shared is a problem halved.

MARCH

FRIDAY 19

My **power** word today is:

Choose a word from the power words on p460

My three most important tasks:

My other tasks:

My wish list:

Notes/reminders:

6am

7am

8am

9am

10am

11am

12 noon

1pm

2pm

3pm

4pm

5pm

6pm

7pm

8pm

9pm

10pm

Today I am grateful for:

Today I accomplished:

Any action is better than no action.

SATURDAY 20

My **power** word today is:

Choose a word from the power words on p460

SUNDAY 21

My **power** word today is:

Choose a word from the power words on p460

Soup up your self esteem.

MARCH

MONDAY 22

This week's focus:

My **power** word today is:

Choose a word from the power words on p460

My three most important tasks:

My other tasks:

My wish list:

Notes/reminders:

6am

7am

8am

9am

10am

11am

12 noon

1pm

2pm

3pm

4pm

5pm

6pm

7pm

8pm

9pm

10pm

Today I am grateful for:

Today I accomplished:

Your challenge may be someone else's opportunity.

MARCH

TUESDAY 23

My **power** word today is:

Choose a word from the power words on p460

My three most important tasks:

My other tasks:

My wish list:

Notes/reminders:

6am

7am

8am

9am

10am

11am

12 noon

1pm

2pm

3pm

4pm

5pm

6pm

7pm

8pm

9pm

10pm

Today I am grateful for:

Today I accomplished:

Don't compare yourself with others.

MARCH

WEDNESDAY 24

My **power** word today is:

Choose a word from the power words on p460

My three most important tasks:

My other tasks:

My wish list:

Notes/reminders:

6am

7am

8am

9am

10am

11am

12 noon

1pm

2pm

3pm

4pm

5pm

6pm

7pm

8pm

9pm

10pm

Today I am grateful for:

Today I accomplished:

Be an effective team player.

MARCH

THURSDAY 25

My power word today is:

Choose a word from the power words on p460

My three most important tasks:

My other tasks:

My wish list:

Notes/reminders:

6am

7am

8am

9am

10am

11am

12 noon

1pm

2pm

3pm

4pm

5pm

6pm

7pm

8pm

9pm

10pm

Today I am grateful for:

Today I accomplished:

Master the basic skill of good communication – listening!

MARCH

FRIDAY 26

My power word today is:

Choose a word from the power words on p460

My three most important tasks:

My other tasks:

My wish list:

Notes/reminders:

6am

7am

8am

9am

10am

11am

12 noon

1pm

2pm

3pm

4pm

5pm

6pm

7pm

8pm

9pm

10pm

Today I am grateful for:

Today I accomplished:

Stay calm.

SATURDAY 27

My **power** word today is:

Choose a word from the power words on p460

SUNDAY 28

My **power** word today is:

Choose a word from the power words on p460

Keep learning.

MARCH

MONDAY 29

This week's focus:

My power word today is:

Choose a word from the power words on p460

My three most important tasks:

My other tasks:

My wish list:

Notes/reminders:

6am

7am

8am

9am

10am

11am

12 noon

1pm

2pm

3pm

4pm

5pm

6pm

7pm

8pm

9pm

10pm

Today I am grateful for:

Today I accomplished:

Decide what is important to you.

MARCH

TUESDAY 30

My power word today is:

Choose a word from the power words on p460

My three most important tasks:

My other tasks:

My wish list:

Notes/reminders:

6am

7am

8am

9am

10am

11am

12 noon

1pm

2pm

3pm

4pm

5pm

6pm

7pm

8pm

9pm

10pm

Today I am grateful for:

Today I accomplished:

Don't settle for someone else's definition of you.

MARCH

WEDNESDAY 31

My power word today is:

Choose a word from the power words on p460

on p460

6am

7am

8am

9am

10am

11am

12 noon

1pm

2pm

3pm

4pm

5pm

6pm

7pm

8pm

9pm

10pm

My three most important tasks:

My other tasks:

My wish list:

Notes/reminders:

Today I am grateful for:

Today I accomplished:

Keep your desk tidy.

21 WAYS TO KEEP YOUR RELATIONSHIP
STRONG

Make your relationship a priority.
Accept that disappointments will happen.
Practice forgiveness.
Be generous with admiration and compliments.
Engage in meaningful conversation.
Let go of the desire to fix or change your partner.
Accept responsibility for how you show up in your relationship.
Focus on the qualities you love and respect in your partner.
Trust that your partner has good intentions.
Learn how to be fully present.
Bring your best to the relationship.
Make it clear that you want to hear and understand your partner.
Be open and share what is important to you.
Ask your partner to share what is important to them.
In a dispute, give the relationship a vote.
Learn what needs to happen for your partner to feel loved and respected.
Understand we all have baggage – best to leave it behind.
Respect each others' boundaries.
Respect yourself and express your thoughts and feelings openly.
Beware of keeping secrets 'to protect' your partner!
Own your own limiting beliefs.
Be true to your word.
Take the time to express appreciation.
Daydream together.

MARCH

Monthly reflections

Do not follow where the path may lead. Go instead where there is no path and leave a trail.
Ralph Waldo Emerson

Best moments:

Greatest accomplishments:

Toughest challenge:

Biggest learnings:

Progress towards ongoing goals:

Remember your 2021 promises and your BIG WHY.
Remind yourself of your motives on page 10.

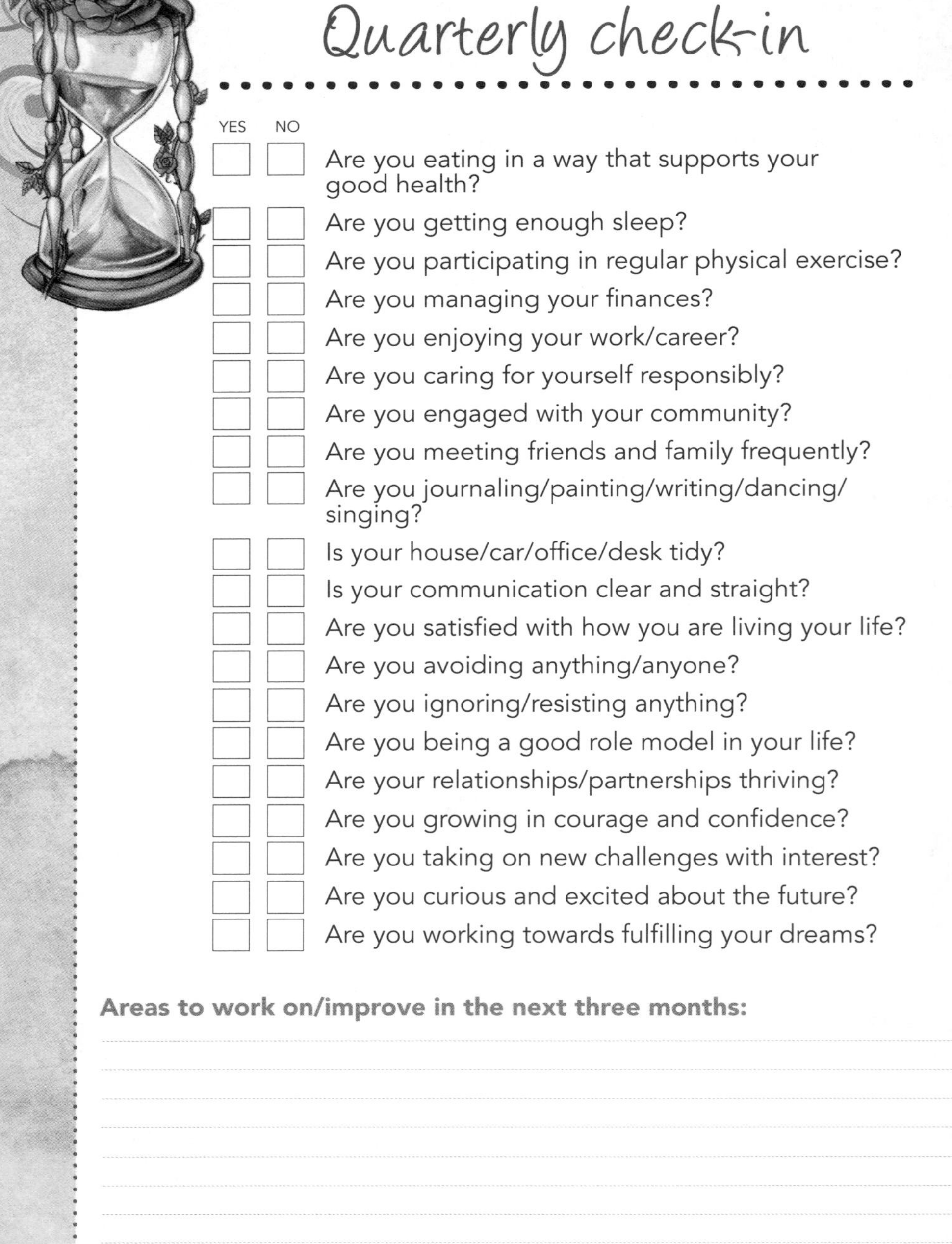

Quarterly check-in

YES	NO	
☐	☐	Are you eating in a way that supports your good health?
☐	☐	Are you getting enough sleep?
☐	☐	Are you participating in regular physical exercise?
☐	☐	Are you managing your finances?
☐	☐	Are you enjoying your work/career?
☐	☐	Are you caring for yourself responsibly?
☐	☐	Are you engaged with your community?
☐	☐	Are you meeting friends and family frequently?
☐	☐	Are you journaling/painting/writing/dancing/singing?
☐	☐	Is your house/car/office/desk tidy?
☐	☐	Is your communication clear and straight?
☐	☐	Are you satisfied with how you are living your life?
☐	☐	Are you avoiding anything/anyone?
☐	☐	Are you ignoring/resisting anything?
☐	☐	Are you being a good role model in your life?
☐	☐	Are your relationships/partnerships thriving?
☐	☐	Are you growing in courage and confidence?
☐	☐	Are you taking on new challenges with interest?
☐	☐	Are you curious and excited about the future?
☐	☐	Are you working towards fulfilling your dreams?

Areas to work on/improve in the next three months:

APRIL

Take the first step in faith.
You don't have to see the whole staircase.
Just take the first step.

Dr Martin Luther King Jr

APRIL AT A GLANCE

MONDAY	TUESDAY	WEDNESDAY	THURSDAY	FRIDAY	SATURDAY	SUNDAY
			1	2	3	4
5	6	7	8	9	10	11
12	13	14	15	16	17	18
19	20	21	22	23	24	25
26	27	28	29	30		

APRIL ACTION PLANNER

A goal is a dream with a deadline

Dates/days to celebrate:

Events to attend:

People to meet/follow up:

Appointments to keep:

Trips to plan:

Purchases/payments to make:

Friends/family to contact:

Movies to see/books to read:

APRIL

Monthly motivator

PRIORITIES

GOALS

CHALLENGES

ACTIONS

APRIL

Financial tracker

MONTHLY CASH FLOW

	Personal	Business	Total
Income			
Salary			
Business dividend			
Pension			
Subsidy			
Other			
Total			
Living expenses			
Mortgage/rent			
Utilities/bills			
Credit card payments			
Loan repayments			
Insurance (home/car/life/health)			
Tax (personal/car/property)			
Savings			
Pension/investments			
House/garden			
Travel/fuel			
Groceries/toiletries			
Entertainment/dining out			
Education/training			
Child care			
Home care			
Health/self care/gym			
Other			
Total			
Total income			
Total outgoings			
Surplus/deficit			
This month's priority			

APRIL

Food planner

An apple a day keeps the doctor away.
Proverb

MY MENU PLANNER (grocery list)

Week 1

Week 2

Week 3

Week 4

Reflections and comments:

This month's meal ideas:

All the money in the world can't buy you back good health.
Reba McEntire

MY HEALTHY NUTRITION PLAN

	BREAKFAST	LUNCH	DINNER	SNACKS	FRUIT	VEGETABLES	WATER
Week 1							
Week 2							
Week 3							
Week 4							

Reflections and comments:

This month's healthy eating ideas:

APRIL

Health planner

Health is not simply the absence of sickness.
Hannah Green

MY EXERCISE PLAN

	ACTIVITY	DURATION	HR	WT/BMI	NOTES
Week 1					
Week 2					
Week 3					
Week 4					

Reflections and comments:

This month's fitness goal:

A good laugh and a long sleep are the best cures in the doctor's book.
Irish proverb

MY WELLBEING PLAN

	PHYSICAL	MENTAL/EMOTIONAL	SOCIAL	FINANCIAL
Week 1				
Week 2				
Week 3				
Week 4				

Reflections and comments:

This month's wellbeing goal:

APRIL

Doodles and ideas

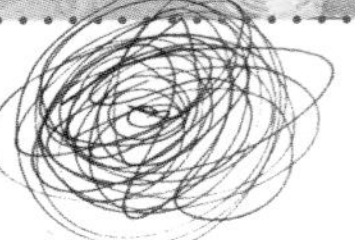

5 TIPS FOR SUCCESS

- Love what you do
- Don't compare
- Help others
- Stay focused
- Persevere

I PROMISE MYSELF

To be so strong that nothing can disturb my peace of mind. **To talk health**, happiness and prosperity to every person I meet. **To make all my friends feel** that there is something worthwhile in them. **To look at the sunny side** of everything and make my optimism come true. **To think only of the best**, to work only for the best and to expect only the best. **To be just as enthusiastic** about the success of others as I am about my own. **To forget the mistakes** of the past and press on to the greater achievements of the future. **To wear a cheerful expression** at all times and give a smile to every living creature I meet. **To give so much time** to improving myself that I have no time to criticise others. **To be too large for worry**, too noble for anger, too strong for fear and too happy to permit the presence of trouble. **To think well of myself** and to proclaim this fact to the world, not in loud words, but in great deeds. **To live in faith** that the whole world is on my side, so long as I am true to the best that there is in me.

Christian D Larson

It's nonsense to be afraid of others' opinions. Some people may think you crazy, while others may think you're a legend. You're the only one who's opinion of you matters.

APRIL

THURSDAY 1

My **power** word today is:

Choose a word from the power words on p460

My three most important tasks:

My other tasks:

My wish list:

Notes/reminders:

6am

7am

8am

9am

10am

11am

12 noon

1pm

2pm

3pm

4pm

5pm

6pm

7pm

8pm

9pm

10pm

Today I am grateful for:

Today I accomplished:

Compliment others.

APRIL • Good Friday

FRIDAY 2

My **power** word today is:

Choose a word from the power words on p460

My three most important tasks:

My other tasks:

My wish list:

Notes/reminders:

6am

7am

8am

9am

10am

11am

12 noon

1pm

2pm

3pm

4pm

5pm

6pm

7pm

8pm

9pm

10pm

Today I am grateful for:

Today I accomplished:

Don't be talking when you should be listening.

SATURDAY 3

My **power** word today is:

Choose a word from the power words on p460

SUNDAY 4 Easter Sunday

My **power** word today is:

Choose a word from the power words on p460

There's no calories in chocolate on Easter Sunday!

APRIL • Easter Monday

MONDAY 5

This week's focus:

My **power** word today is:

Choose a word from the power words on p460

My three most important tasks:

My other tasks:

My wish list:

Notes/reminders:

6am

7am

8am

9am

10am

11am

12 noon

1pm

2pm

3pm

4pm

5pm

6pm

7pm

8pm

9pm

10pm

Today I am grateful for:

Today I accomplished:

Encourage and help others to succeed.

APRIL

TUESDAY 6

My **power** word today is:

Choose a word from the power words on p460

My three most important tasks:

My other tasks:

My wish list:

Notes/reminders:

6am

7am

8am

9am

10am

11am

12 noon

1pm

2pm

3pm

4pm

5pm

6pm

7pm

8pm

9pm

10pm

Today I am grateful for:

Today I accomplished:

See the funny side.

APRIL

WEDNESDAY 7

My **power** word today is:

Choose a word from the power words on p460

My three most important tasks:

My other tasks:

My wish list:

Notes/reminders:

6am

7am

8am

9am

10am

11am

12 noon

1pm

2pm

3pm

4pm

5pm

6pm

7pm

8pm

9pm

10pm

Today I am grateful for:

Today I accomplished:

Good habits will give you positive results.

APRIL

THURSDAY 8

My **power** word today is:

Choose a word from the power words on p460

My three most important tasks:

My other tasks:

My wish list:

Notes/reminders:

6am

7am

8am

9am

10am

11am

12 noon

1pm

2pm

3pm

4pm

5pm

6pm

7pm

8pm

9pm

10pm

Today I am grateful for:

Today I accomplished:

Apply the 80/20 principle.

APRIL

FRIDAY 9

My **power** word today is:

Choose a word from the power words on p460

My three most important tasks:

My other tasks:

My wish list:

Notes/reminders:

6am

7am

8am

9am

10am

11am

12 noon

1pm

2pm

3pm

4pm

5pm

6pm

7pm

8pm

9pm

10pm

Today I am grateful for:

Today I accomplished:

Be grateful.

SATURDAY 10

My **power** word today is:

Choose a word from the power words on p460

SUNDAY 11

My **power** word today is:

Choose a word from the power words on p460

Give credit where credit is due.

APRIL

MONDAY 12

This week's focus:

My **power** word today is:

Choose a word from the power words on p460

My three most important tasks:

My other tasks:

My wish list:

Notes/reminders:

6am

7am

8am

9am

10am

11am

12 noon

1pm

2pm

3pm

4pm

5pm

6pm

7pm

8pm

9pm

10pm

Today I am grateful for:

Today I accomplished:

Find time to exercise daily.

APRIL

TUESDAY 13

My **power** word today is:

Choose a word from the power words on p460

My three most important tasks:

My other tasks:

My wish list:

Notes/reminders:

6am

7am

8am

9am

10am

11am

12 noon

1pm

2pm

3pm

4pm

5pm

6pm

7pm

8pm

9pm

10pm

Today I am grateful for:

Today I accomplished:

Listen to inspirational people.

APRIL

WEDNESDAY 14

My **power** word today is:

Choose a word from the power words on p460

My three most important tasks:

My other tasks:

My wish list:

Notes/reminders:

6am

7am

8am

9am

10am

11am

12 noon

1pm

2pm

3pm

4pm

5pm

6pm

7pm

8pm

9pm

10pm

Today I am grateful for:

Today I accomplished:

Break big tasks into little tasks.

APRIL

THURSDAY 15

My **power** word today is:

Choose a word from the power words on p460

My three most important tasks:

My other tasks:

My wish list:

Notes/reminders:

6am

7am

8am

9am

10am

11am

12 noon

1pm

2pm

3pm

4pm

5pm

6pm

7pm

8pm

9pm

10pm

Today I am grateful for:

Today I accomplished:

Give up being negative.

APRIL

FRIDAY 16

My **power** word today is:

Choose a word from the power words on p460

6am

7am

8am

9am

10am

11am

12 noon

1pm

2pm

3pm

4pm

5pm

6pm

7pm

8pm

9pm

10pm

My three most important tasks:

My other tasks:

My wish list:

Notes/reminders:

Today I am grateful for:

Today I accomplished:

Avoid self defeating self talk.

SATURDAY 17

My **power** word today is:

Choose a word from the power words on p460

SUNDAY 18

My **power** word today is:

Choose a word from the power words on p460

Be responsible for your own results.

APRIL

MONDAY 19

This week's focus:

My **power** word today is:

Choose a word from the power words on p460

6am

7am

8am

9am

10am

11am

12 noon

1pm

2pm

3pm

4pm

5pm

6pm

7pm

8pm

9pm

10pm

My three most important tasks:

My other tasks:

My wish list:

Notes/reminders:

Today I am grateful for:

Today I accomplished:

Stop doing what doesn't work.

APRIL

TUESDAY 20

My **power** word today is:

Choose a word from the power words on p460

My three most important tasks:

My other tasks:

My wish list:

Notes/reminders:

6am

7am

8am

9am

10am

11am

12 noon

1pm

2pm

3pm

4pm

5pm

6pm

7pm

8pm

9pm

10pm

Today I am grateful for:

Today I accomplished:

Quit complaining.

APRIL

WEDNESDAY 21

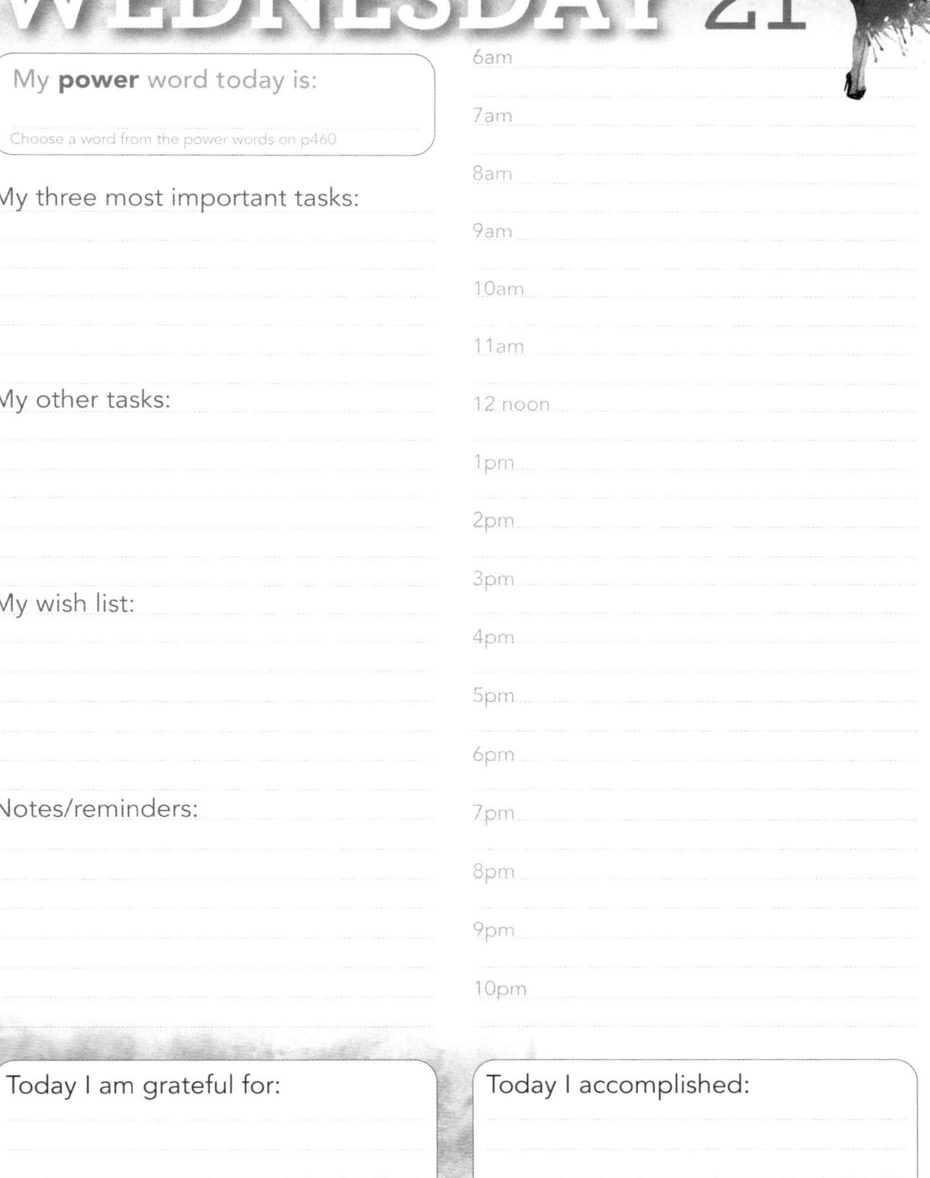

My **power** word today is:

Choose a word from the power words on p460

My three most important tasks:

My other tasks:

My wish list:

Notes/reminders:

6am

7am

8am

9am

10am

11am

12 noon

1pm

2pm

3pm

4pm

5pm

6pm

7pm

8pm

9pm

10pm

Today I am grateful for:

Today I accomplished:

Discover the power of visualisation.

THURSDAY 22

My **power** word today is:

Choose a word from the power words on p460

My three most important tasks:

My other tasks:

My wish list:

Notes/reminders:

6am

7am

8am

9am

10am

11am

12 noon

1pm

2pm

3pm

4pm

5pm

6pm

7pm

8pm

9pm

10pm

Today I am grateful for:

Today I accomplished:

Develop new habits.

APRIL

FRIDAY 23

My **power** word today is:

Choose a word from the power words on p460

My three most important tasks:

My other tasks:

My wish list:

Notes/reminders:

6am

7am

8am

9am

10am

11am

12 noon

1pm

2pm

3pm

4pm

5pm

6pm

7pm

8pm

9pm

10pm

Today I am grateful for:

Today I accomplished:

Widen your social circle.

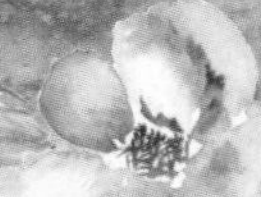

SATURDAY 24

My **power** word today is:

Choose a word from the power words on p460

SUNDAY 25

My **power** word today is:

Choose a word from the power words on p460

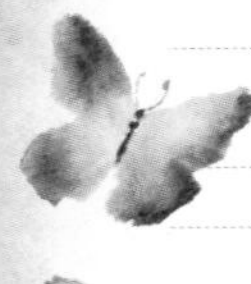

Expect and embrace change.

APRIL

MONDAY 26

This week's focus:

My **power** word today is:

Choose a word from the power words on p460

My three most important tasks:

My other tasks:

My wish list:

Notes/reminders:

6am

7am

8am

9am

10am

11am

12 noon

1pm

2pm

3pm

4pm

5pm

6pm

7pm

8pm

9pm

10pm

Today I am grateful for:

Today I accomplished:

Use affirmations to empower yourself.

APRIL

TUESDAY 27

My **power** word today is:

Choose a word from the power words on p460

My three most important tasks:

My other tasks:

My wish list:

Notes/reminders:

6am

7am

8am

9am

10am

11am

12 noon

1pm

2pm

3pm

4pm

5pm

6pm

7pm

8pm

9pm

10pm

Today I am grateful for:

Today I accomplished:

Spend time with happy people.

APRIL

WEDNESDAY 28

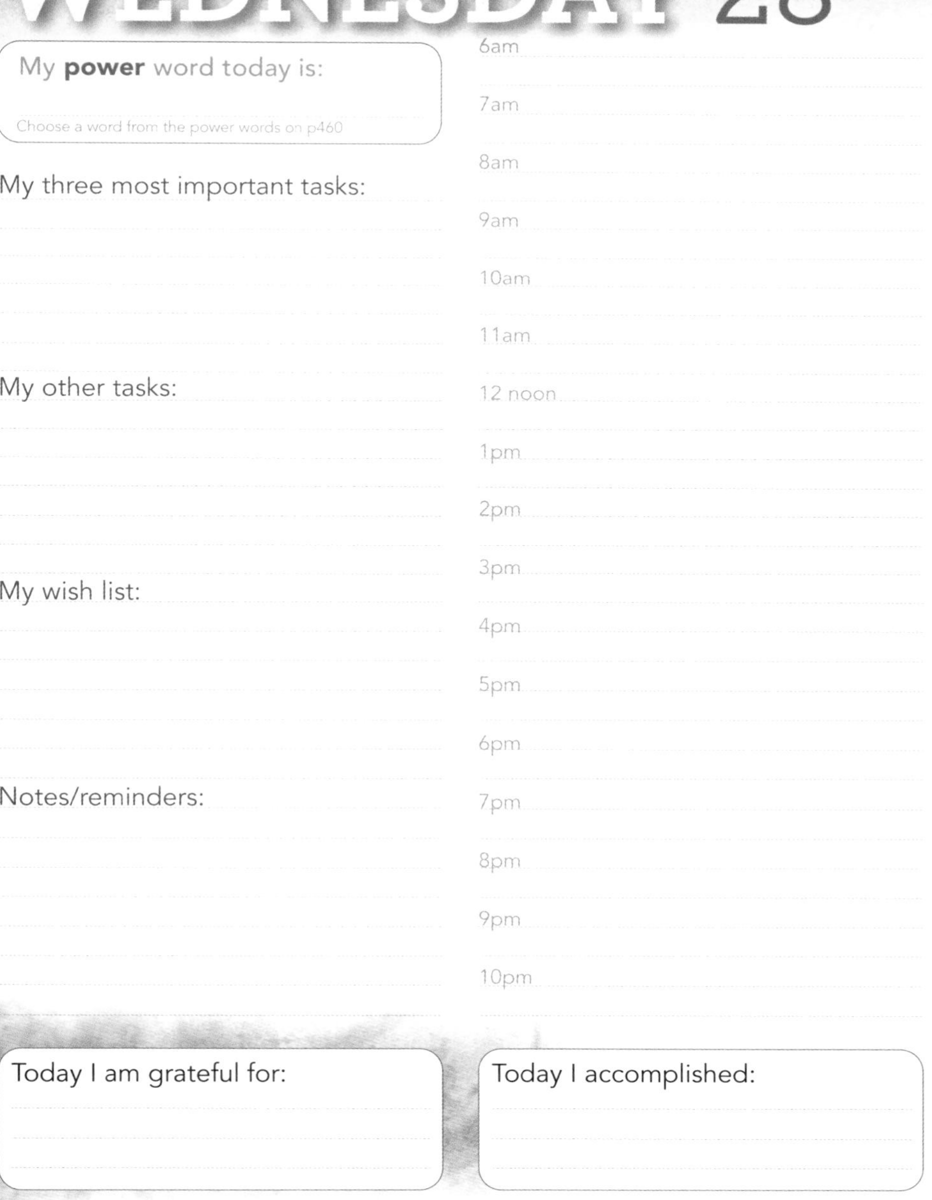

Today I am grateful for:

Today I accomplished:

Decide your own value and don't sell yourself short.

APRIL

THURSDAY 29

My **power** word today is:

Choose a word from the power words on p460

My three most important tasks:

My other tasks:

My wish list:

Notes/reminders:

6am

7am

8am

9am

10am

11am

12 noon

1pm

2pm

3pm

4pm

5pm

6pm

7pm

8pm

9pm

10pm

Today I am grateful for:

Today I accomplished:

Share ideas and information.

APRIL

FRIDAY 30

My **power** word today is:

Choose a word from the power words on p460

My three most important tasks:

My other tasks:

My wish list:

Notes/reminders:

6am

7am

8am

9am

10am

11am

12 noon

1pm

2pm

3pm

4pm

5pm

6pm

7pm

8pm

9pm

10pm

Today I am grateful for:

Today I accomplished:

Accept that we each have different strengths and talents .

APRIL

Monthly reflections

Start where you are. Use what you have. Do what you can.
Arthur Ashe

Best moments:

Greatest accomplishments:

Toughest challenge:

Biggest learnings:

Progress towards ongoing goals:

Remember your 2021 promises and your BIG WHY.
Remind yourself of your motives on page 10.

MAY

Imagination is everything. It is the preview of life's coming attractions.

Albert Einstein

MAY
AT A GLANCE

MONDAY	TUESDAY	WEDNESDAY	THURSDAY	FRIDAY	SATURDAY	SUNDAY
					1	2
3	4	5	6	7	8	9
10	11	12	13	14	15	16
17	18	19	20	21	22	23
24	25	26	27	28	29	30
31						

MAY ACTION PLANNER

A goal is a dream with a deadline

Dates/days to celebrate:

Events to attend:

People to meet/follow up:

Appointments to keep:

Trips to plan:

Purchases/payments to make:

Friends/family to contact:

Movies to see/books to read:

MAY

Monthly motivator

PRIORITIES

GOALS

CHALLENGES

ACTIONS

MAY

Financial tracker

MONTHLY CASH FLOW

	Personal	Business	Total
Income			
Salary			
Business dividend			
Pension			
Subsidy			
Other			
Total			
Living expenses			
Mortgage/rent			
Utilities/bills			
Credit card payments			
Loan repayments			
Insurance (home/car/life/health)			
Tax (personal/car/property)			
Savings			
Pension/investments			
House/garden			
Travel/fuel			
Groceries/toiletries			
Entertainment/dining out			
Education/training			
Child care			
Home care			
Health/self care/gym			
Other			
Total			
Total income			
Total outgoings			
Surplus/deficit			
This month's priority			

Food planner

True healthcare reform starts in your kitchen.

MY MENU PLANNER (grocery list)

Week 1

Week 2

Week 3

Week 4

Reflections and comments:

This month's meal ideas:

If you don't do what's best for your body, you're the one who comes up on the short end.
Julius Erving

MY HEALTHY NUTRITION PLAN

	BREAKFAST	LUNCH	DINNER	SNACKS	FRUIT	VEGETABLES	WATER
Week 1							
Week 2							
Week 3							
Week 4							

Reflections and comments:

This month's healthy eating ideas:

Health planner

Take care of your body. It's the only place you have to live.
Jim Rohn

MY EXERCISE PLAN

	ACTIVITY	DURATION	HR	WT/BMI	NOTES
Week 1					
Week 2					
Week 3					
Week 4					

Reflections and comments:

This month's fitness goal:

Happiness is nothing more than good health and a bad memory.
Albert Schweitzer

MY WELLBEING PLAN

	PHYSICAL	MENTAL/EMOTIONAL	SOCIAL	FINANCIAL
Week 1				
Week 2				
Week 3				
Week 4				

Reflections and comments:

This month's wellbeing goal:

MAY

Doodles and ideas

5 TIPS FOR GOOD HEALTH

- Plenty of exercise and water
- Maintain a healthy weight
- Eat natural foods
- Be optimistic
- Avoid unhealthy habits

Whatever you can do, or dream, begin it. Boldness has genius, power and magic in it.

Johann Wolfgang von Goethe

36 things everyone should know how to do

SELF RELIANCE IS A VITAL KEY TO LIVING A HEALTHY PRODUCTIVE LIFE

1. Write a letter
2. Use a computer
3. Follow basic instructions
4. Perform basic first aid
5. Drive a car
6. Do basic cooking
7. Have a party piece
8. Deliver bad news
9. Handle a job interview
10. Manage time
11. Remember names
12. Travel light
13. Book a flight
14. Give directions
15. Swim
16. Recognise alcohol limits
17. Select good produce
18. Handle a hammer
19. Make a simple budget
20. Follow a simple exercise program
21. Negotiate
22. Give a sincere compliment
23. Listen carefully to others
24. Paint a room
25. Deliver a short presentation
26. Smile at the camera
27. Take useful notes
28. Mind your own business
29. Be a good house guest
30. Read a map
31. Protect personal information
32. Recognise a scam
33. Laugh at yourself
34. Keep a house clean
35. Hold a baby
36. Remove a stain

MAY

SATURDAY 1

My **power** word today is:

Choose a word from the power words on p460

SUNDAY 2

My **power** word today is:

Choose a word from the power words on p460

Get a good night's sleep.

MAY • Bank Holiday

MONDAY 3

This week's focus:

My **power** word today is:

Choose a word from the power words on p460

6am

7am

8am

9am

10am

11am

12 noon

1pm

2pm

3pm

4pm

5pm

6pm

7pm

8pm

9pm

10pm

My three most important tasks:

My other tasks:

My wish list:

Notes/reminders:

Today I am grateful for:

Today I accomplished:

Stand your ground.

MAY

TUESDAY 4

My **power** word today is:

Choose a word from the power words on p460

My three most important tasks:

My other tasks:

My wish list:

Notes/reminders:

6am

7am

8am

9am

10am

11am

12 noon

1pm

2pm

3pm

4pm

5pm

6pm

7pm

8pm

9pm

10pm

Today I am grateful for:

Today I accomplished:

Don't be afraid to take risks.

MAY

WEDNESDAY 5

My **power** word today is:

Choose a word from the power words on p460

My three most important tasks:

My other tasks:

My wish list:

Notes/reminders:

6am

7am

8am

9am

10am

11am

12 noon

1pm

2pm

3pm

4pm

5pm

6pm

7pm

8pm

9pm

10pm

Today I am grateful for:

Today I accomplished:

What you discover for yourself is yours forever.

MAY

THURSDAY 6

My **power** word today is:

Choose a word from the power words on p460

My three most important tasks:

My other tasks:

My wish list:

Notes/reminders:

6am

7am

8am

9am

10am

11am

12 noon

1pm

2pm

3pm

4pm

5pm

6pm

7pm

8pm

9pm

10pm

Today I am grateful for:

Today I accomplished:

Have confidence in your ability to add value to the world.

MAY

FRIDAY 7

My **power** word today is:

Choose a word from the power words on p460

My three most important tasks:

My other tasks:

My wish list:

Notes/reminders:

6am

7am

8am

9am

10am

11am

12 noon

1pm

2pm

3pm

4pm

5pm

6pm

7pm

8pm

9pm

10pm

Today I am grateful for:

Today I accomplished:

Smile, it lights up your face.

MAY

SATURDAY 8

My **power** word today is:

Choose a word from the power words on p460

SUNDAY 9

My **power** word today is:

Choose a word from the power words on p460

Tomorrow is another day.

MAY

MONDAY 10

This week's focus:

My **power** word today is:

Choose a word from the power words on p460

My three most important tasks:

My other tasks:

My wish list:

Notes/reminders:

6am

7am

8am

9am

10am

11am

12 noon

1pm

2pm

3pm

4pm

5pm

6pm

7pm

8pm

9pm

10pm

Today I am grateful for:

Today I accomplished:

Write a letter to your future self.

MAY

TUESDAY 11

My **power** word today is:

Choose a word from the power words on p460

My three most important tasks:

My other tasks:

My wish list:

Notes/reminders:

6am

7am

8am

9am

10am

11am

12 noon

1pm

2pm

3pm

4pm

5pm

6pm

7pm

8pm

9pm

10pm

Today I am grateful for:

Today I accomplished:

Seek first to understand.

MAY

WEDNESDAY 12

My **power** word today is:

Choose a word from the power words on p460

My three most important tasks:

My other tasks:

My wish list:

Notes/reminders:

6am

7am

8am

9am

10am

11am

12 noon

1pm

2pm

3pm

4pm

5pm

6pm

7pm

8pm

9pm

10pm

Today I am grateful for:

Today I accomplished:

Mind your moods.

MAY

THURSDAY 13

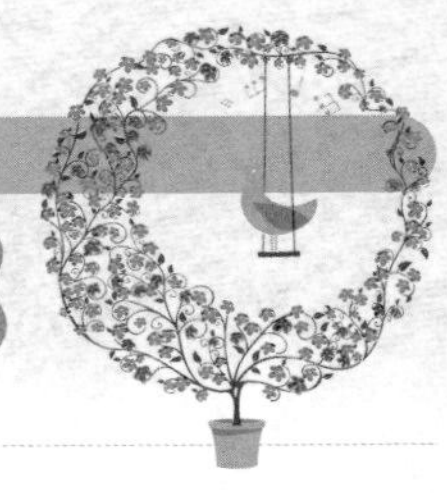

My **power** word today is:

Choose a word from the power words on p460

My three most important tasks:

My other tasks:

My wish list:

Notes/reminders:

6am

7am

8am

9am

10am

11am

12 noon

1pm

2pm

3pm

4pm

5pm

6pm

7pm

8pm

9pm

10pm

Today I am grateful for:

Today I accomplished:

Fix the problem, not the blame.

MAY

FRIDAY 14

My **power** word today is:

Choose a word from the power words on p460

My three most important tasks:

My other tasks:

My wish list:

Notes/reminders:

6am

7am

8am

9am

10am

11am

12 noon

1pm

2pm

3pm

4pm

5pm

6pm

7pm

8pm

9pm

10pm

Today I am grateful for:

Today I accomplished:

Everyone has a different point of view.

SATURDAY 15

My **power** word today is:

Choose a word from the power words on p460

SUNDAY 16

My **power** word today is:

Choose a word from the power words on p460

Feel the fear and do it anyway.

MAY

MONDAY 17

This week's focus:

My **power** word today is:

Choose a word from the power words on p460

My three most important tasks:

My other tasks:

My wish list:

Notes/reminders:

6am

7am

8am

9am

10am

11am

12 noon

1pm

2pm

3pm

4pm

5pm

6pm

7pm

8pm

9pm

10pm

Today I am grateful for:

Today I accomplished:

You are loved.

MAY

TUESDAY 18

My **power** word today is:

Choose a word from the power words on p460

My three most important tasks:

My other tasks:

My wish list:

Notes/reminders:

6am

7am

8am

9am

10am

11am

12 noon

1pm

2pm

3pm

4pm

5pm

6pm

7pm

8pm

9pm

10pm

Today I am grateful for:

Today I accomplished:

Fortune favours the brave.

MAY

WEDNESDAY 19

My **power** word today is:

Choose a word from the power words on p460

My three most important tasks:

My other tasks:

My wish list:

Notes/reminders:

6am

7am

8am

9am

10am

11am

12 noon

1pm

2pm

3pm

4pm

5pm

6pm

7pm

8pm

9pm

10pm

Today I am grateful for:

Today I accomplished:

With the new day comes new strength.

MAY

THURSDAY 20

My **power** word today is:

Choose a word from the power words on p460

My three most important tasks:

My other tasks:

My wish list:

Notes/reminders:

6am

7am

8am

9am

10am

11am

12 noon

1pm

2pm

3pm

4pm

5pm

6pm

7pm

8pm

9pm

10pm

Today I am grateful for:

Today I accomplished:

Speak as if what you say is important. It is.

MAY

FRIDAY 21

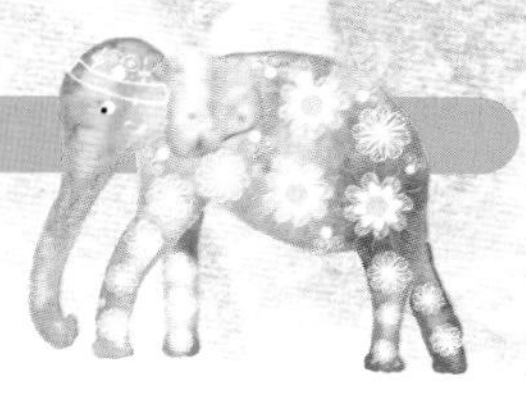

My **power** word today is:

Choose a word from the power words on p460

My three most important tasks:

My other tasks:

My wish list:

Notes/reminders:

6am

7am

8am

9am

10am

11am

12 noon

1pm

2pm

3pm

4pm

5pm

6pm

7pm

8pm

9pm

10pm

Today I am grateful for:

Today I accomplished:

Believe in yourself.

SATURDAY 22

My **power** word today is:

Choose a word from the power words on p460

SUNDAY 23

My **power** word today is:

Choose a word from the power words on p460

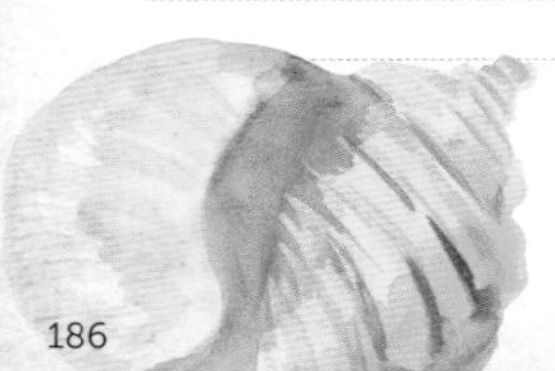

To try is to succeed.

MAY

MONDAY 24

This week's focus:

My **power** word today is:

Choose a word from the power words on p460

My three most important tasks:

My other tasks:

My wish list:

Notes/reminders:

6am

7am

8am

9am

10am

11am

12 noon

1pm

2pm

3pm

4pm

5pm

6pm

7pm

8pm

9pm

10pm

Today I am grateful for:

Today I accomplished:

The only limits are in your mind.

MAY

TUESDAY 25

My **power** word today is:

Choose a word from the power words on p460

My three most important tasks:

My other tasks:

My wish list:

Notes/reminders:

6am

7am

8am

9am

10am

11am

12 noon

1pm

2pm

3pm

4pm

5pm

6pm

7pm

8pm

9pm

10pm

Today I am grateful for:

Today I accomplished:

Have confidence in your decisions.

MAY

WEDNESDAY 26

My **power** word today is:

Choose a word from the power words on p460

My three most important tasks:

My other tasks:

My wish list:

Notes/reminders:

6am

7am

8am

9am

10am

11am

12 noon

1pm

2pm

3pm

4pm

5pm

6pm

7pm

8pm

9pm

10pm

Today I am grateful for:

Today I accomplished:

Every cloud has a silver lining.

MAY

THURSDAY 27

My **power** word today is:

Choose a word from the power words on p460

My three most important tasks:

My other tasks:

My wish list:

Notes/reminders:

6am

7am

8am

9am

10am

11am

12 noon

1pm

2pm

3pm

4pm

5pm

6pm

7pm

8pm

9pm

10pm

Today I am grateful for:

Today I accomplished:

Be good to yourself.

MAY

FRIDAY 28

My **power** word today is:

Choose a word from the power words on p460

My three most important tasks:

My other tasks:

My wish list:

Notes/reminders:

6am

7am

8am

9am

10am

11am

12 noon

1pm

2pm

3pm

4pm

5pm

6pm

7pm

8pm

9pm

10pm

Today I am grateful for:

Today I accomplished:

You will never regret doing your best.

MAY

SATURDAY 29

My **power** word today is:

Choose a word from the power words on p460

SUNDAY 30

My **power** word today is:

Choose a word from the power words on p460

Don't hide your light under a bushel.

MAY

MONDAY 31

This week's focus:

My **power** word today is:

Choose a word from the power words on p460

My three most important tasks:

My other tasks:

My wish list:

Notes/reminders:

6am

7am

8am

9am

10am

11am

12 noon

1pm

2pm

3pm

4pm

5pm

6pm

7pm

8pm

9pm

10pm

Today I am grateful for:

Today I accomplished:

Be clear on your future vision.

Monthly reflections

Never limit yourself because of others' limited imagination; never limit others because of your own limited imagination.

Mae Jemison

Best moments:

Greatest accomplishments:

Toughest challenge:

Biggest learnings:

Progress towards ongoing goals:

Remember your 2021 promises and your BIG WHY.

Remind yourself of your motives on page 10.

DESIDERATA

Go placidly amid the noise and haste, and remember what peace there may be in silence. As far as possible without surrender be on good terms with all persons. Speak your truth quietly and clearly, and listen to others, even the dull and ignorant; they too have their story.

Avoid loud and aggressive persons, they are vexations to the spirit. If you compare yourself with others, you may become vain and bitter; for always there will be greater and lesser persons than yourself. Enjoy your achievements as well as your plans. Keep interested in your own career, however humble; it is a real possession in the changing fortunes of time. Exercise caution in your business affairs; for the world is full of trickery. But let this not blind you to what virtue there is; many persons strive for high ideals; and everywhere life is full of heroism.

Be yourself. Especially, do not feign affection. Neither be cynical about love; for in the face of all aridity and disenchantment it is perennial as the grass. Take kindly the counsel of the years, gracefully surrendering the things of youth. Nurture strength of spirit to shield you in sudden misfortune. But do not distress yourself with imaginings. Many fears are born of fatigue and loneliness. Beyond a wholesome discipline, be gentle with yourself.

You are a child of the universe, no less than the trees and the stars; you have a right to be here. And whether or not it is clear to you, no doubt the universe is unfolding as it should. Therefore be at peace with God, whatever you conceive him to be; and whatever your labours and aspirations, in the noisy confusion of life keep peace with your soul. With all its sham, drudgery and broken dreams, it is still a beautiful world.
Be cheerful. Strive to be happy.

Max Ehrmann

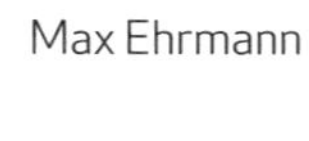

PERSONAL AFFIRMATIONS

I am

I can

I will

I am

I can

I will

I am

I can

I will

I am

I can

I will

I am

I can

I will

FUTURE VISION

Fast forward one year from now

Look back on the past year and fill in what happened.
Use your best imagination. Go for what you truly want.

I AM SO GRATEFUL FOR THE PAST YEAR

In the past year: ....

My health: ....

My family: ....

My friends: ....

My living situation: ....

My time: ....

My team: ....

My work: ....

My income: ....

My network: ....

My mentors: ....

My pastimes: ....

My passions: ....

My contribution: ....

My sense of purpose: ....

My accomplishments: ....

My proudest moment: ....

My vision: ....

My upcoming year: ....

When you have completed your future vision, how inspired do you feel on a scale of 1-10? ....

Keep updating it until you are 10/10. ....

Check in with page 92 and update your vision board.

When the vision of your future is more compelling than the memories of your past, your life will change.

Roger James Hamilton

SLOW DANCE

Have you ever watched kids on a merry-go-round?
Or listened to the rain slapping the ground?
Ever followed a butterfly's erratic flight?
Or gazed at the sun into the fading night?
You better slow down
Don't dance so fast.
Time is short.
The music won't last.
Do you run through each day on the fly?
When you ask: How are you? do you hear the reply?
When the day is done, do you lie in your bed
With the next hundred chores running through your head?
You'd better slow down.
Don't dance so fast.
Time is short.
The music won't last.
Ever told your child, we'll do it tomorrow?
And in your haste, not see his sorrow?
Ever lost touch, let a good friendship die
Cause you never had time to call and say, "Hi"?
You'd better slow down
Don't dance so fast.
Time is short.
The music won't last.
When you run so fast to get somewhere
You miss half the fun of getting there.
When you worry and hurry through the day,
It's like an unopened gift thrown away.
Life is not a race.
Do take it slower.
Hear the music
Before the song is over.

David L Weatherford

JUNE

How wonderful it is that nobody need wait a single moment before starting to improve the world.

Anne Frank

JUNE

AT A GLANCE

MONDAY	TUESDAY	WEDNESDAY	THURSDAY	FRIDAY	SATURDAY	SUNDAY
	1	2	3	4	5	6
7	8	9	10	11	12	13
14	15	16	17	18	19	20
21	22	23	24	25	26	27
28	29	30				

JUNE ACTION PLANNER

Dates/days to celebrate:

Events to attend:

People to meet/follow up:

Appointments to keep:

Trips to plan:

Purchases/payments to make:

Friends/family to contact:

Movies to see/books to read:

JUNE

Monthly motivator

PRIORITIES

GOALS

CHALLENGES

ACTIONS

JUNE

Financial tracker

MONTHLY CASH FLOW

	Personal	Business	Total
Income			
Salary			
Business dividend			
Pension			
Subsidy			
Other			
Total			
Living expenses			
Mortgage/rent			
Utilities/bills			
Credit card payments			
Loan repayments			
Insurance (home/car/life/health)			
Tax (personal/car/property)			
Savings			
Pension/investments			
House/garden			
Travel/fuel			
Groceries/toiletries			
Entertainment/dining out			
Education/training			
Child care			
Home care			
Health/self care/gym			
Other			
Total			
Total income			
Total outgoings			
Surplus/deficit			
This month's priority			

JUNE

Food planner

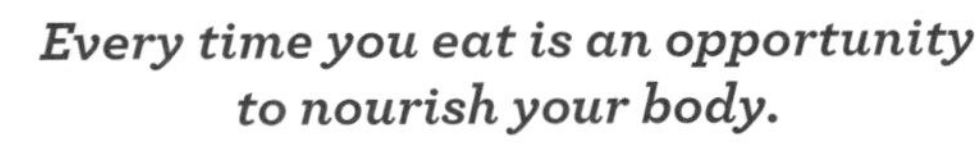

Every time you eat is an opportunity to nourish your body.

MY MENU PLANNER (grocery list)

Week 1

Week 2

Week 3

Week 4

Reflections and comments:

This month's meal ideas:

Life expectancy would grow by leaps and bounds if green vegetables smelled as good as bacon.

Doug Larson

MY HEALTHY NUTRITION PLAN

	BREAKFAST	LUNCH	DINNER	SNACKS	FRUIT	VEGETABLES	WATER
Week 1							
Week 2							
Week 3							
Week 4							

Reflections and comments:

This month's healthy eating ideas:

JUNE

Health planner

An ounce of prevention is worth a pound of cure.

MY EXERCISE PLAN

	ACTIVITY	DURATION	HR	WT/BMI	NOTES
Week 1					
Week 2					
Week 3					
Week 4					

Reflections and comments:

This month's fitness goal:

A calm mind brings inner strength and self-confidence, both very important for good health.

MY WELLBEING PLAN

	PHYSICAL	MENTAL/EMOTIONAL	SOCIAL	FINANCIAL
Week 1				
Week 2				
Week 3				
Week 4				

Reflections and comments:

This month's wellbeing goal:

JUNE

Doodles and ideas

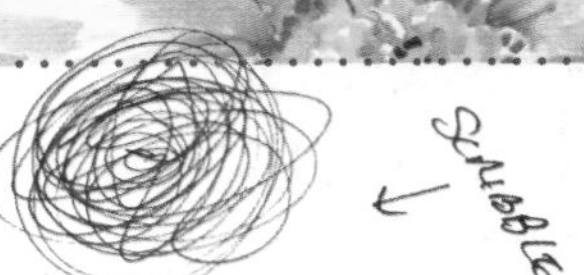

5 TIPS FOR GREAT RELATIONSHIPS

- Listen generously
- Share openly
- Promise faithfully
- Encourage freely
- Live honestly

JUNE

TUESDAY 1

My **power** word today is:

Choose a word from the power words on p460

My three most important tasks:

My other tasks:

My wish list:

Notes/reminders:

6am

7am

8am

9am

10am

11am

12 noon

1pm

2pm

3pm

4pm

5pm

6pm

7pm

8pm

9pm

10pm

Today I am grateful for:

Today I accomplished:

Look beyond appearances.

JUNE

WEDNESDAY 2

My **power** word today is:

Choose a word from the power words on p460

My three most important tasks:

My other tasks:

My wish list:

Notes/reminders:

6am

7am

8am

9am

10am

11am

12 noon

1pm

2pm

3pm

4pm

5pm

6pm

7pm

8pm

9pm

10pm

Today I am grateful for:

Today I accomplished:

Don't sell yourself short.

JUNE

THURSDAY 3

My **power** word today is:

Choose a word from the power words on p460

My three most important tasks:

My other tasks:

My wish list:

Notes/reminders:

6am

7am

8am

9am

10am

11am

12 noon

1pm

2pm

3pm

4pm

5pm

6pm

7pm

8pm

9pm

10pm

Today I am grateful for:

Today I accomplished:

It pays to hold your nerve.

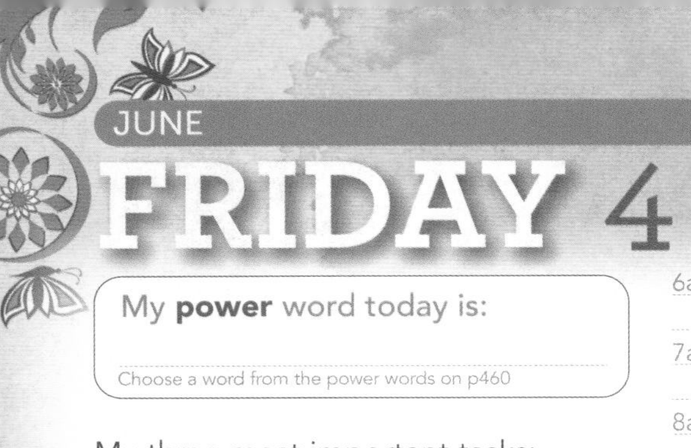

JUNE

FRIDAY 4

My **power** word today is:

Choose a word from the power words on p460

My three most important tasks:

My other tasks:

My wish list:

Notes/reminders:

6am

7am

8am

9am

10am

11am

12 noon

1pm

2pm

3pm

4pm

5pm

6pm

7pm

8pm

9pm

10pm

Today I am grateful for:

Today I accomplished:

Act ethically and sleep easily.

JUNE

SATURDAY 5

My **power** word today is:

Choose a word from the power words on p460

SUNDAY 6

My **power** word today is:

Choose a word from the power words on p460

Look for a unique solution.

JUNE • Bank Holiday

MONDAY 7

This week's focus:

My **power** word today is:

Choose a word from the power words on p460

My three most important tasks:

My other tasks:

My wish list:

Notes/reminders:

6am

7am

8am

9am

10am

11am

12 noon

1pm

2pm

3pm

4pm

5pm

6pm

7pm

8pm

9pm

10pm

Today I am grateful for:

Today I accomplished:

Set high standards for yourself.

JUNE

TUESDAY 8

My **power** word today is:

Choose a word from the power words on p460

My three most important tasks:

My other tasks:

My wish list:

Notes/reminders:

6am

7am

8am

9am

10am

11am

12 noon

1pm

2pm

3pm

4pm

5pm

6pm

7pm

8pm

9pm

10pm

Today I am grateful for:

Today I accomplished:

Be clear on your core values.

JUNE

WEDNESDAY 9

My **power** word today is:

Choose a word from the power words on p460

My three most important tasks:

My other tasks:

My wish list:

Notes/reminders:

6am

7am

8am

9am

10am

11am

12 noon

1pm

2pm

3pm

4pm

5pm

6pm

7pm

8pm

9pm

10pm

Today I am grateful for:

Today I accomplished:

Lead by example.

JUNE

THURSDAY 10

My **power** word today is:

Choose a word from the power words on p460

My three most important tasks:

My other tasks:

My wish list:

Notes/reminders:

6am

7am

8am

9am

10am

11am

12 noon

1pm

2pm

3pm

4pm

5pm

6pm

7pm

8pm

9pm

10pm

Today I am grateful for:

Today I accomplished:

Reputation is everything.

JUNE

FRIDAY 11

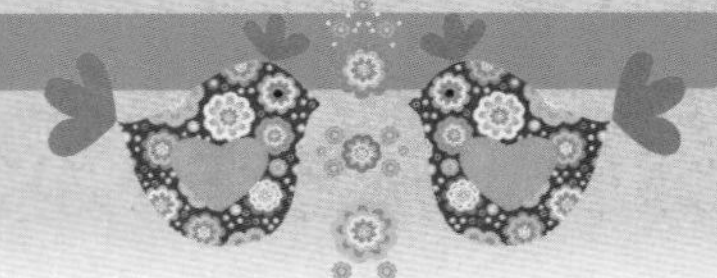

My **power** word today is:

Choose a word from the power words on p460

My three most important tasks:

My other tasks:

My wish list:

Notes/reminders:

6am

7am

8am

9am

10am

11am

12 noon

1pm

2pm

3pm

4pm

5pm

6pm

7pm

8pm

9pm

10pm

Today I am grateful for:

Today I accomplished:

Learn what you can from 'failure' and move on.

SATURDAY 12

My **power** word today is:

Choose a word from the power words on p460

SUNDAY 13

My **power** word today is:

Choose a word from the power words on p460

Act with integrity.

JUNE

MONDAY 14

This week's focus:

My **power** word today is:

Choose a word from the power words on p460

My three most important tasks:

My other tasks:

My wish list:

Notes/reminders:

6am

7am

8am

9am

10am

11am

12 noon

1pm

2pm

3pm

4pm

5pm

6pm

7pm

8pm

9pm

10pm

Today I am grateful for:

Today I accomplished:

Focus on the greater good.

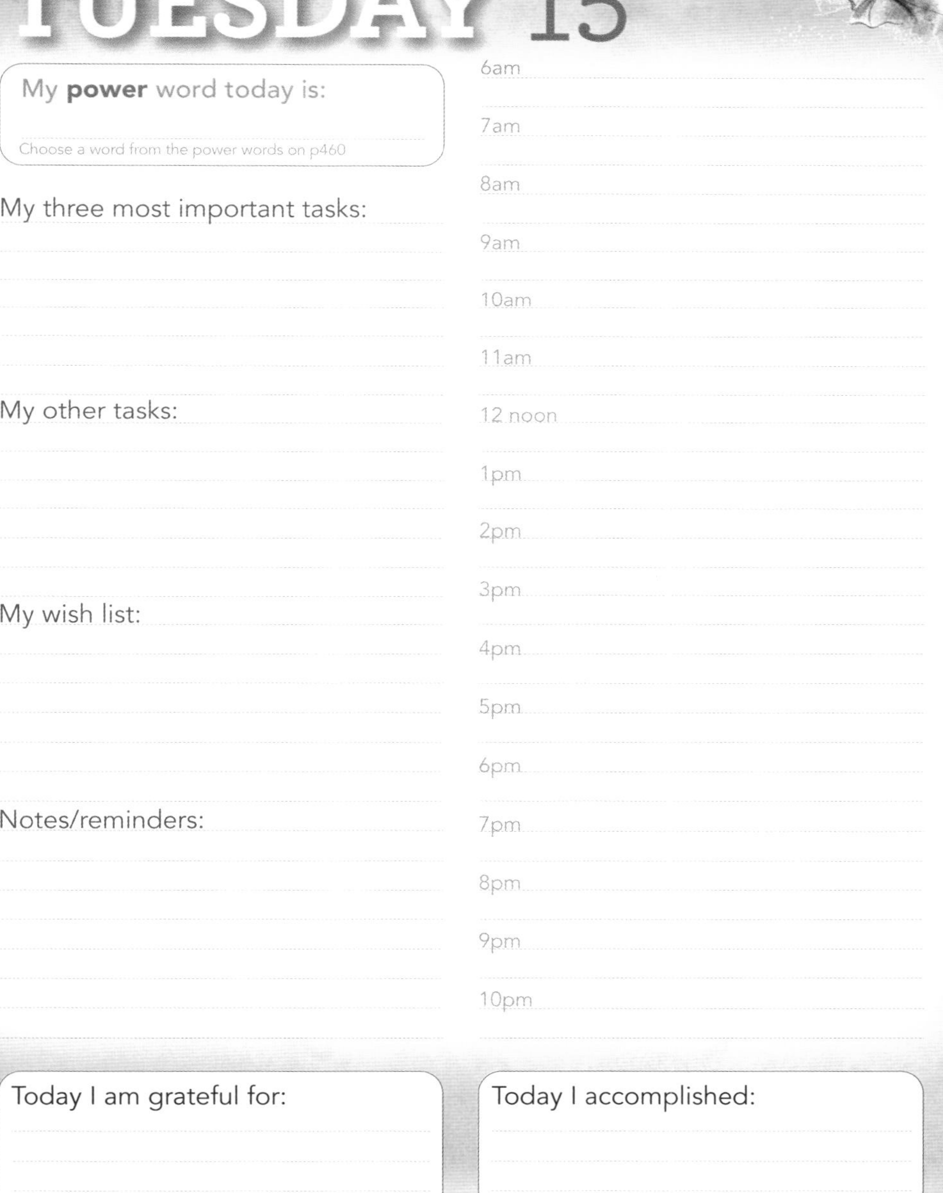

JUNE

TUESDAY 15

My **power** word today is:

Choose a word from the power words on p460

My three most important tasks:

My other tasks:

My wish list:

Notes/reminders:

6am

7am

8am

9am

10am

11am

12 noon

1pm

2pm

3pm

4pm

5pm

6pm

7pm

8pm

9pm

10pm

Today I am grateful for:

Today I accomplished:

Principles matter.

JUNE

WEDNESDAY 16

My **power** word today is:

Choose a word from the power words on p460

My three most important tasks:

My other tasks:

My wish list:

Notes/reminders:

6am

7am

8am

9am

10am

11am

12 noon

1pm

2pm

3pm

4pm

5pm

6pm

7pm

8pm

9pm

10pm

Today I am grateful for:

Today I accomplished:

It's OK to pursue excellence.

JUNE

THURSDAY 17

My **power** word today is:

Choose a word from the power words on p460

My three most important tasks:

My other tasks:

My wish list:

Notes/reminders:

6am

7am

8am

9am

10am

11am

12 noon

1pm

2pm

3pm

4pm

5pm

6pm

7pm

8pm

9pm

10pm

Today I am grateful for:

Today I accomplished:

Good advice never gets old.

JUNE

FRIDAY 18

My **power** word today is:

Choose a word from the power words on p460

My three most important tasks:

My other tasks:

My wish list:

Notes/reminders:

6am

7am

8am

9am

10am

11am

12 noon

1pm

2pm

3pm

4pm

5pm

6pm

7pm

8pm

9pm

10pm

Today I am grateful for:

Today I accomplished:

Have a clear vision for your future – visualise it to realise it.

SATURDAY 19

My **power** word today is:

Choose a word from the power words on p460

SUNDAY 20

Happy Father's Day!

My **power** word today is:

Choose a word from the power words on p460

Never stop learning.

JUNE

MONDAY 21

This week's focus:

My **power** word today is:

Choose a word from the power words on p460

6am

7am

8am

9am

10am

11am

12 noon

1pm

2pm

3pm

4pm

5pm

6pm

7pm

8pm

9pm

10pm

My three most important tasks:

My other tasks:

My wish list:

Notes/reminders:

Today I am grateful for:

Today I accomplished:

In times of confusion, go back to basics.

JUNE

TUESDAY 22

My **power** word today is:

Choose a word from the power words on p460

My three most important tasks:

My other tasks:

My wish list:

Notes/reminders:

6am

7am

8am

9am

10am

11am

12 noon

1pm

2pm

3pm

4pm

5pm

6pm

7pm

8pm

9pm

10pm

Today I am grateful for:

Today I accomplished:

Never underestimate the importance of showing up.

JUNE

WEDNESDAY 23

My **power** word today is:

Choose a word from the power words on p460

My three most important tasks:

My other tasks:

My wish list:

Notes/reminders:

6am

7am

8am

9am

10am

11am

12 noon

1pm

2pm

3pm

4pm

5pm

6pm

7pm

8pm

9pm

10pm

Today I am grateful for:

Today I accomplished:

There is no need to reinvent the wheel.

JUNE

THURSDAY 24

My **power** word today is:

Choose a word from the power words on p460

My three most important tasks:

My other tasks:

My wish list:

Notes/reminders:

6am

7am

8am

9am

10am

11am

12 noon

1pm

2pm

3pm

4pm

5pm

6pm

7pm

8pm

9pm

10pm

Today I am grateful for:

Today I accomplished:

Consider collaboration instead of competition.

JUNE

FRIDAY 25

My **power** word today is:

Choose a word from the power words on p460

My three most important tasks:

My other tasks:

My wish list:

Notes/reminders:

6am

7am

8am

9am

10am

11am

12 noon

1pm

2pm

3pm

4pm

5pm

6pm

7pm

8pm

9pm

10pm

Today I am grateful for:

Today I accomplished:

Think outside the box and colour outside the lines.

SATURDAY 26

My **power** word today is:

Choose a word from the power words on p460

SUNDAY 27

My **power** word today is:

Choose a word from the power words on p460

Make the ordinary in your life, extraordinary.

JUNE

MONDAY 28

This week's focus:

My **power** word today is:

Choose a word from the power words on p460

My three most important tasks:

My other tasks:

My wish list:

Notes/reminders:

6am

7am

8am

9am

10am

11am

12 noon

1pm

2pm

3pm

4pm

5pm

6pm

7pm

8pm

9pm

10pm

Today I am grateful for:

Today I accomplished:

Trust that truth will prevail.

JUNE

TUESDAY 29

My **power** word today is:

Choose a word from the power words on p460

My three most important tasks:

My other tasks:

My wish list:

Notes/reminders:

6am

7am

8am

9am

10am

11am

12 noon

1pm

2pm

3pm

4pm

5pm

6pm

7pm

8pm

9pm

10pm

Today I am grateful for:

Today I accomplished:

Be part of the solution not part of the problem.

JUNE

WEDNESDAY 30

My **power** word today is:

Choose a word from the power words on p460

My three most important tasks:

My other tasks:

My wish list:

Notes/reminders:

6am

7am

8am

9am

10am

11am

12 noon

1pm

2pm

3pm

4pm

5pm

6pm

7pm

8pm

9pm

10pm

Today I am grateful for:

Today I accomplished:

Speak without offending.

JUNE

Monthly reflections

Much of the stress that people feel doesn't come from having too much to do. It comes from not finishing what they started.
David Allen

Best moments:

Greatest accomplishments:

Toughest challenge:

Biggest learnings:

Progress towards ongoing goals:

Remember your 2021 promises and your BIG WHY.
Remind yourself of your motives on page 10.

Quarterly check-in

YES	NO	
☐	☐	Are you eating in a way that supports your good health?
☐	☐	Are you getting enough sleep?
☐	☐	Are you participating in regular physical exercise?
☐	☐	Are you managing your finances?
☐	☐	Are you enjoying your work/career?
☐	☐	Are you caring for yourself responsibly?
☐	☐	Are you engaged with your community?
☐	☐	Are you meeting friends and family frequently?
☐	☐	Are you journaling/painting/writing/dancing/ singing?
☐	☐	Is your house/car/office/desk tidy?
☐	☐	Is your communication clear and straight?
☐	☐	Are you satisfied with how you are living your life?
☐	☐	Are you avoiding anything/anyone?
☐	☐	Are you ignoring/resisting anything?
☐	☐	Are you being a good role model in your life?
☐	☐	Are your relationships/partnerships thriving?
☐	☐	Are you growing in courage and confidence?
☐	☐	Are you taking on new challenges with interest?
☐	☐	Are you curious and excited about the future?
☐	☐	Are you working towards fulfilling your dreams?

Areas to work on/improve in the next three months:

JULY

To accomplish great things we must not only act, but also dream; not only plan, but also believe.

Anatole France

JULY AT A GLANCE

MONDAY	TUESDAY	WEDNESDAY	THURSDAY	FRIDAY	SATURDAY	SUNDAY
			1	2	3	4
5	6	7	8	9	10	11
12	13	14	15	16	17	18
19	20	21	22	23	24	25
26	27	28	29	30	31	

JULY
ACTION PLANNER

A goal is a dream with a deadline

Dates/days to celebrate:

Events to attend:

People to meet/follow up:

Appointments to keep:

Trips to plan:

Purchases/payments to make:

Friends/family to contact:

Movies to see/books to read:

JULY

Monthly motivator

PRIORITIES

GOALS

CHALLENGES

ACTIONS

JULY

Financial tracker

MONTHLY CASH FLOW

	Personal	Business	Total
Income			
Salary			
Business dividend			
Pension			
Subsidy			
Other			
Total			
Living expenses			
Mortgage/rent			
Utilities/bills			
Credit card payments			
Loan repayments			
Insurance (home/car/life/health)			
Tax (personal/car/property)			
Savings			
Pension/investments			
House/garden			
Travel/fuel			
Groceries/toiletries			
Entertainment/dining out			
Education/training			
Child care			
Home care			
Health/self care/gym			
Other			
Total			
Total income			
Total outgoings			
Surplus/deficit			
This month's priority			

JULY

Food planner

Your body is a temple, but only if you treat it as one.
Astrid Alauda

MY MENU PLANNER (grocery list)

Week 1

Week 2

Week 3

Week 4

Reflections and comments:

This month's meal ideas:

He who takes medicine and neglects his diet wastes the skill of his doctors.
Chinese proverb

MY HEALTHY NUTRITION PLAN

	BREAKFAST	LUNCH	DINNER	SNACKS	FRUIT	VEGETABLES	WATER
Week 1							
Week 2							
Week 3							
Week 4							

Reflections and comments:

This month's healthy eating ideas:

JULY

Health planner

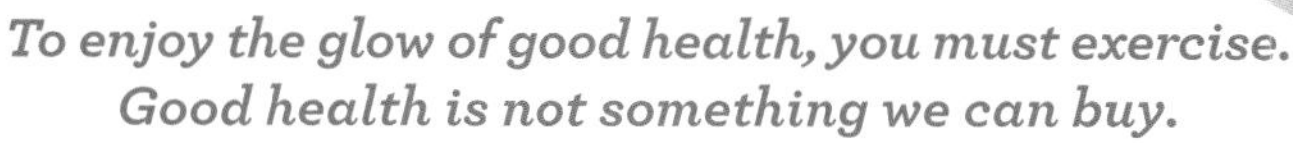
To enjoy the glow of good health, you must exercise.
Good health is not something we can buy.

MY EXERCISE PLAN

	ACTIVITY	DURATION	HR	WT/BMI	NOTES
Week 1					
Week 2					
Week 3					
Week 4					

Reflections and comments:

This month's fitness goal:

A merry heart doeth good like a medicine,
but a broken spirit drieth the bones.

MY WELLBEING PLAN

	PHYSICAL	MENTAL/EMOTIONAL	SOCIAL	FINANCIAL
Week 1				
Week 2				
Week 3				
Week 4				

Reflections and comments:

This month's wellbeing goal:

JULY

Doodles and ideas

Scribble ←

5 TIPS FOR HARMONY IN THE HOME

- Be patient
- Be calm
- Be interested
- Listen
- Share

LETTING GO

To let go does not mean to stop caring,
it means I can't do it for someone else.
To let go is not to cut myself off,
it's the realisation I can't control another.
To let go is not to enable,
but to allow learning from natural consequences.
To let go is to admit powerlessness,
which means the outcome is not in my hands.
To let go is not to try to change or blame another,
it's to make the most of myself.
To let go is not to care for, but to care about.
To let go is not to fix, but to be supportive.
To let go is not to judge,
but to allow another to be a human being.
To let go is not to be in the middle arranging all the
outcomes, but to allow others to affect their destinies.
To let go is not to be protective,
it's to permit another to face reality.
To let go is not to deny, but to accept.
To let go is not to nag, scold or argue, but instead
to search out my own shortcomings and correct them.
To let go is not to adjust everything to my desires,
but to take each day as it comes and cherish myself
in it.
To let go is not to criticise or regulate anybody,
but to try to become what I dream I can be.
To let go is not to regret the past,
but to grow and live for the future.
To let go is to fear less and love more.

JULY

THURSDAY 1

My **power** word today is:

Choose a word from the power words on p460

My three most important tasks:

My other tasks:

My wish list:

Notes/reminders:

6am

7am

8am

9am

10am

11am

12 noon

1pm

2pm

3pm

4pm

5pm

6pm

7pm

8pm

9pm

10pm

Today I am grateful for:

Today I accomplished:

Embrace a can-do attitude.

JULY

FRIDAY 2

My **power** word today is:

Choose a word from the power words on p460

My three most important tasks:

My other tasks:

My wish list:

Notes/reminders:

6am

7am

8am

9am

10am

11am

12 noon

1pm

2pm

3pm

4pm

5pm

6pm

7pm

8pm

9pm

10pm

Today I am grateful for:

Today I accomplished:

Enjoy what you do.

SATURDAY 3

My **power** word today is:

Choose a word from the power words on p460

SUNDAY 4

My **power** word today is:

Choose a word from the power words on p460

Honour your word.

JULY

MONDAY 5

This week's focus:

My **power** word today is:

Choose a word from the power words on p460

My three most important tasks:

My other tasks:

My wish list:

Notes/reminders:

6am

7am

8am

9am

10am

11am

12 noon

1pm

2pm

3pm

4pm

5pm

6pm

7pm

8pm

9pm

10pm

Today I am grateful for:

Today I accomplished:

Don't waste people's time.

JULY

TUESDAY 6

My **power** word today is:

Choose a word from the power words on p460

My three most important tasks:

My other tasks:

My wish list:

Notes/reminders:

6am

7am

8am

9am

10am

11am

12 noon

1pm

2pm

3pm

4pm

5pm

6pm

7pm

8pm

9pm

10pm

Today I am grateful for:

Today I accomplished:

See the opportunity in every challenge.

JULY

WEDNESDAY 7

My **power** word today is:

Choose a word from the power words on p460

My three most important tasks:

My other tasks:

My wish list:

Notes/reminders:

6am

7am

8am

9am

10am

11am

12 noon

1pm

2pm

3pm

4pm

5pm

6pm

7pm

8pm

9pm

10pm

Today I am grateful for:

Today I accomplished:

What we have to learn, we learn by doing.

JULY

THURSDAY 8

My **power** word today is:

Choose a word from the power words on p460

My three most important tasks:

My other tasks:

My wish list:

Notes/reminders:

6am

7am

8am

9am

10am

11am

12 noon

1pm

2pm

3pm

4pm

5pm

6pm

7pm

8pm

9pm

10pm

Today I am grateful for:

Today I accomplished:

Be willing to be held to account.

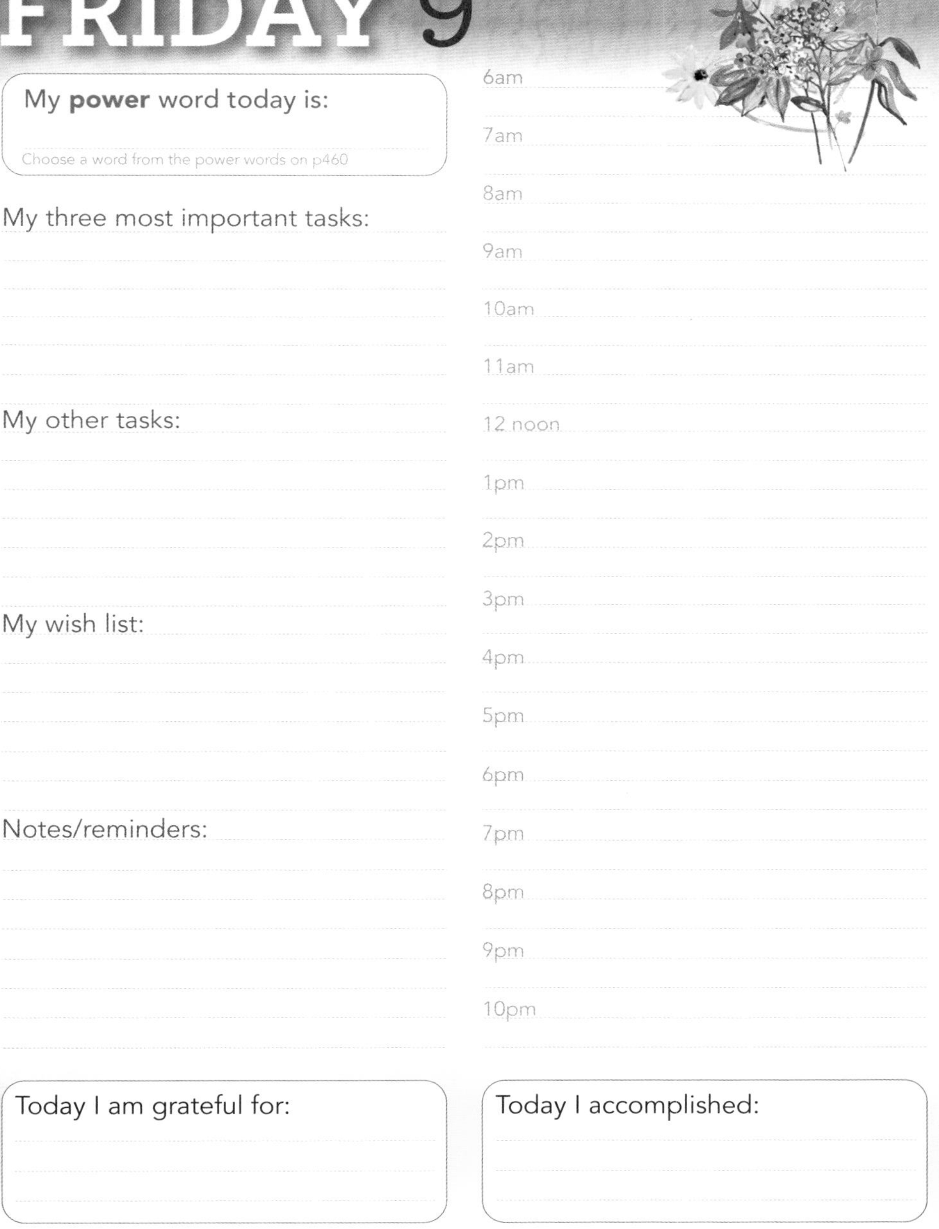

JULY

FRIDAY 9

My **power** word today is:

Choose a word from the power words on p460

My three most important tasks:

My other tasks:

My wish list:

Notes/reminders:

6am

7am

8am

9am

10am

11am

12 noon

1pm

2pm

3pm

4pm

5pm

6pm

7pm

8pm

9pm

10pm

Today I am grateful for:

Today I accomplished:

Freedom brings responsibility.

SATURDAY 10

My **power** word today is:

Choose a word from the power words on p460

SUNDAY 11

My **power** word today is:

Choose a word from the power words on p460

Honesty is always the best policy.

JULY

MONDAY 12

This week's focus:

My **power** word today is:

Choose a word from the power words on p460

My three most important tasks:

My other tasks:

My wish list:

Notes/reminders:

6am

7am

8am

9am

10am

11am

12 noon

1pm

2pm

3pm

4pm

5pm

6pm

7pm

8pm

9pm

10pm

Today I am grateful for:

Today I accomplished:

Let yourself be inspired by great role models.

JULY

TUESDAY 13

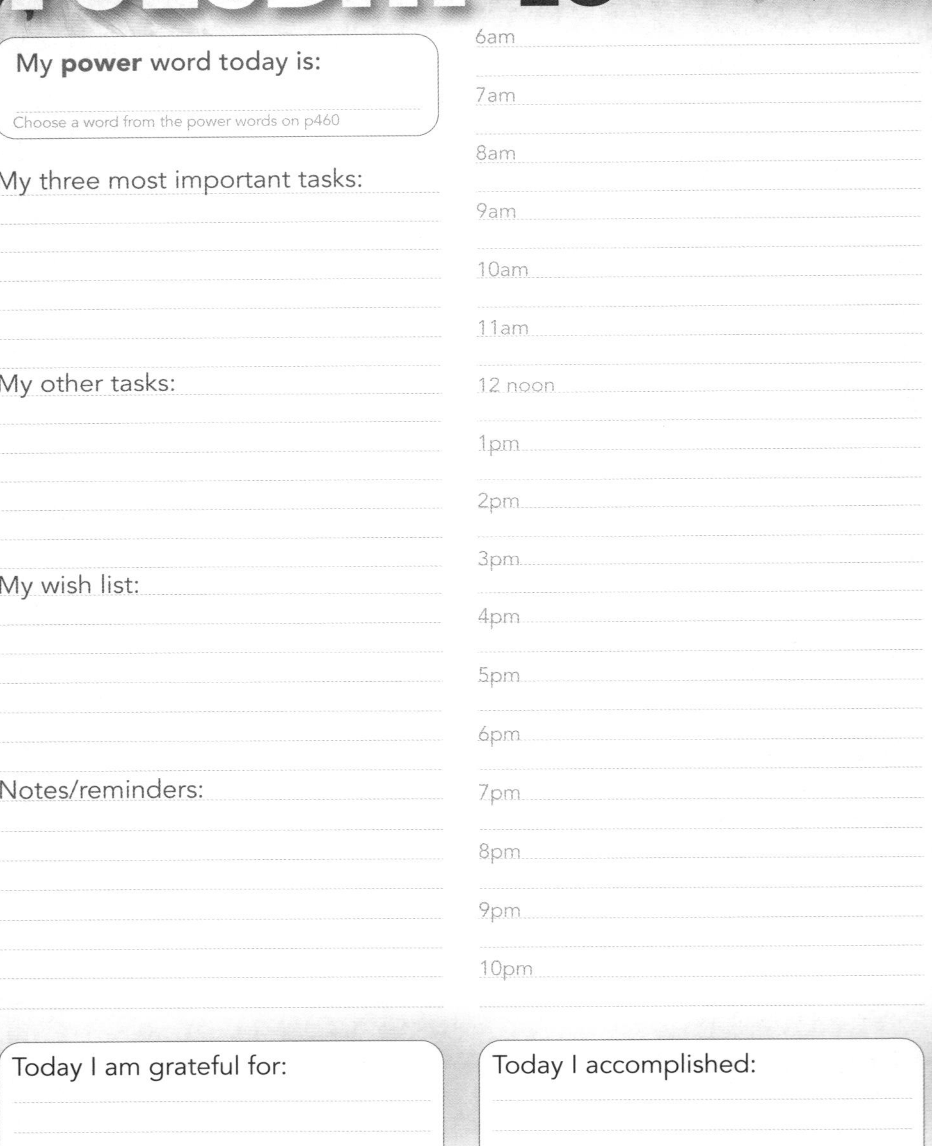

My **power** word today is:

Choose a word from the power words on p460

My three most important tasks:

My other tasks:

My wish list:

Notes/reminders:

6am

7am

8am

9am

10am

11am

12 noon

1pm

2pm

3pm

4pm

5pm

6pm

7pm

8pm

9pm

10pm

Today I am grateful for:

Today I accomplished:

Take an interest in the lives of others.

JULY

WEDNESDAY 14

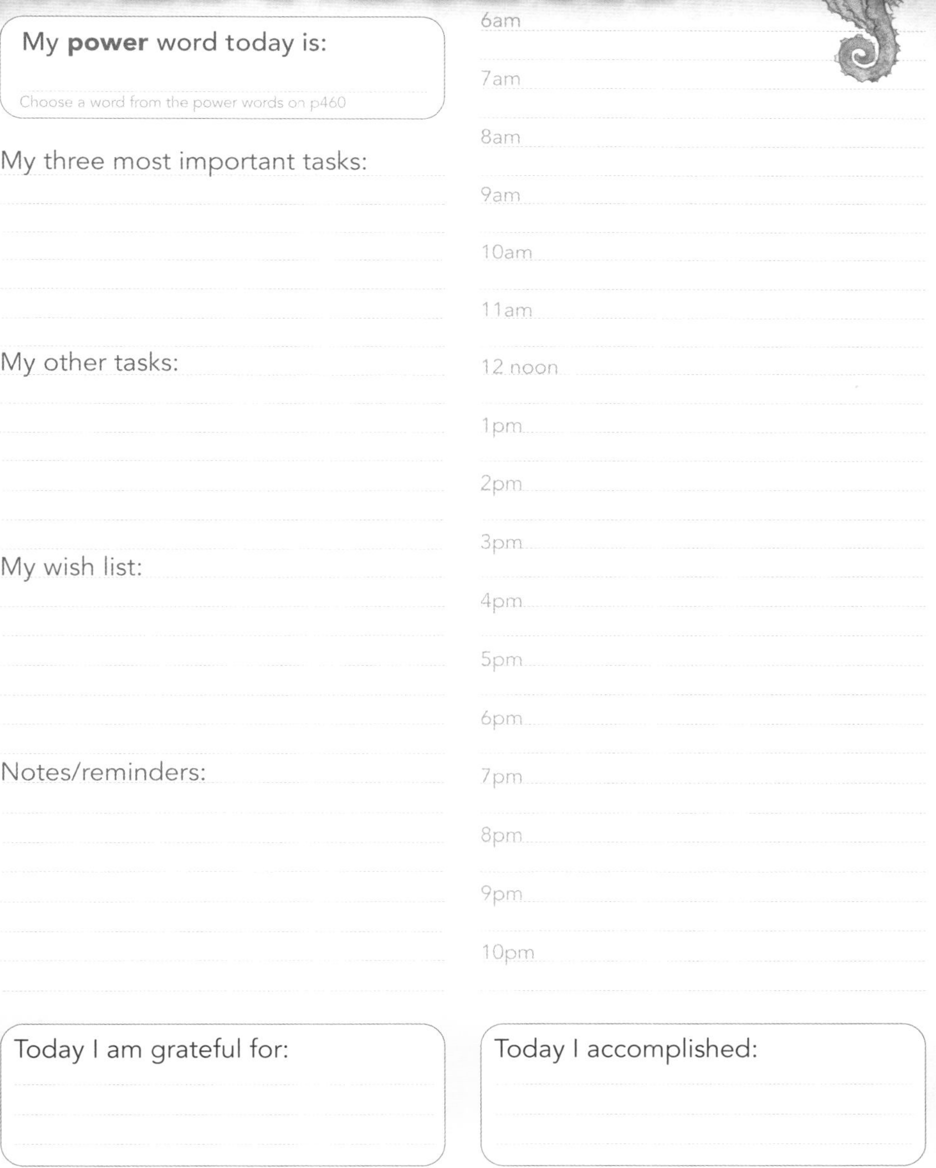

My **power** word today is:

Choose a word from the power words on p460

My three most important tasks:

My other tasks:

My wish list:

Notes/reminders:

6am

7am

8am

9am

10am

11am

12 noon

1pm

2pm

3pm

4pm

5pm

6pm

7pm

8pm

9pm

10pm

Today I am grateful for:

Today I accomplished:

Each person is the architect of their own destiny.

JULY

THURSDAY 15

My **power** word today is:

Choose a word from the power words on p460

My three most important tasks:

My other tasks:

My wish list:

Notes/reminders:

6am

7am

8am

9am

10am

11am

12 noon

1pm

2pm

3pm

4pm

5pm

6pm

7pm

8pm

9pm

10pm

Today I am grateful for:

Today I accomplished:

There will always be consequences.

JULY

FRIDAY 16

My **power** word today is:

Choose a word from the power words on p460

My three most important tasks:

My other tasks:

My wish list:

Notes/reminders:

6am

7am

8am

9am

10am

11am

12 noon

1pm

2pm

3pm

4pm

5pm

6pm

7pm

8pm

9pm

10pm

Today I am grateful for:

Today I accomplished:

Acknowledge others for the talents they have .

JULY

SATURDAY 17

My **power** word today is:

Choose a word from the power words on p460

SUNDAY 18

My **power** word today is:

Choose a word from the power words on p460

Be fully committed to your own personal growth.

JULY

MONDAY 19

This week's focus:

My **power** word today is:

Choose a word from the power words on p460

My three most important tasks:

My other tasks:

My wish list:

Notes/reminders:

6am
7am
8am
9am
10am
11am
12 noon
1pm
2pm
3pm
4pm
5pm
6pm
7pm
8pm
9pm
10pm

Today I am grateful for:

Today I accomplished:

Energy creates energy.

JULY

TUESDAY 20

My **power** word today is:

Choose a word from the power words on p460

My three most important tasks:

My other tasks:

My wish list:

Notes/reminders:

6am

7am

8am

9am

10am

11am

12 noon

1pm

2pm

3pm

4pm

5pm

6pm

7pm

8pm

9pm

10pm

Today I am grateful for:

Today I accomplished:

Humour is a true test of friendship.

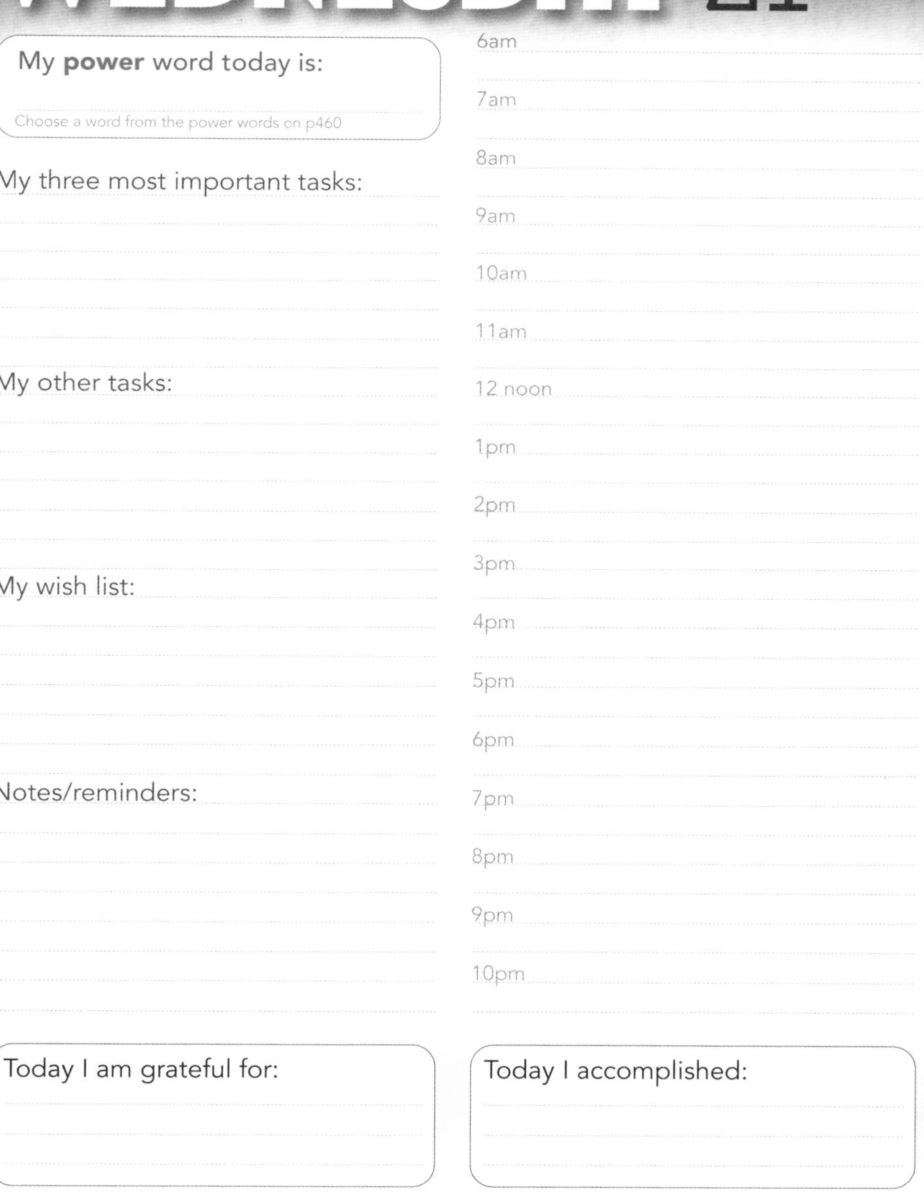

JULY

WEDNESDAY 21

My **power** word today is:

Choose a word from the power words on p460

My three most important tasks:

My other tasks:

My wish list:

Notes/reminders:

6am

7am

8am

9am

10am

11am

12 noon

1pm

2pm

3pm

4pm

5pm

6pm

7pm

8pm

9pm

10pm

Today I am grateful for:

Today I accomplished:

Bring people together.

JULY

THURSDAY 22

My **power** word today is:

Choose a word from the power words on p460

My three most important tasks:

My other tasks:

My wish list:

Notes/reminders:

6am

7am

8am

9am

10am

11am

12 noon

1pm

2pm

3pm

4pm

5pm

6pm

7pm

8pm

9pm

10pm

Today I am grateful for:

Today I accomplished:

Give up the need to control.

JULY

FRIDAY 23

My **power** word today is:

Choose a word from the power words on p460

My three most important tasks:

My other tasks:

My wish list:

Notes/reminders:

6am

7am

8am

9am

10am

11am

12 noon

1pm

2pm

3pm

4pm

5pm

6pm

7pm

8pm

9pm

10pm

Today I am grateful for:

Today I accomplished:

When you feel down, look up to the stars.

JULY

SATURDAY 24

My **power** word today is:

Choose a word from the power words on p460

SUNDAY 25

My **power** word today is:

Choose a word from the power words on p460

Stay true to yourself.

JULY

MONDAY 26

This week's focus:

My **power** word today is:

Choose a word from the power words on p460

My three most important tasks:

My other tasks:

My wish list:

Notes/reminders:

6am

7am

8am

9am

10am

11am

12 noon

1pm

2pm

3pm

4pm

5pm

6pm

7pm

8pm

9pm

10pm

Today I am grateful for:

Today I accomplished:

Be on time.

JULY

TUESDAY 27

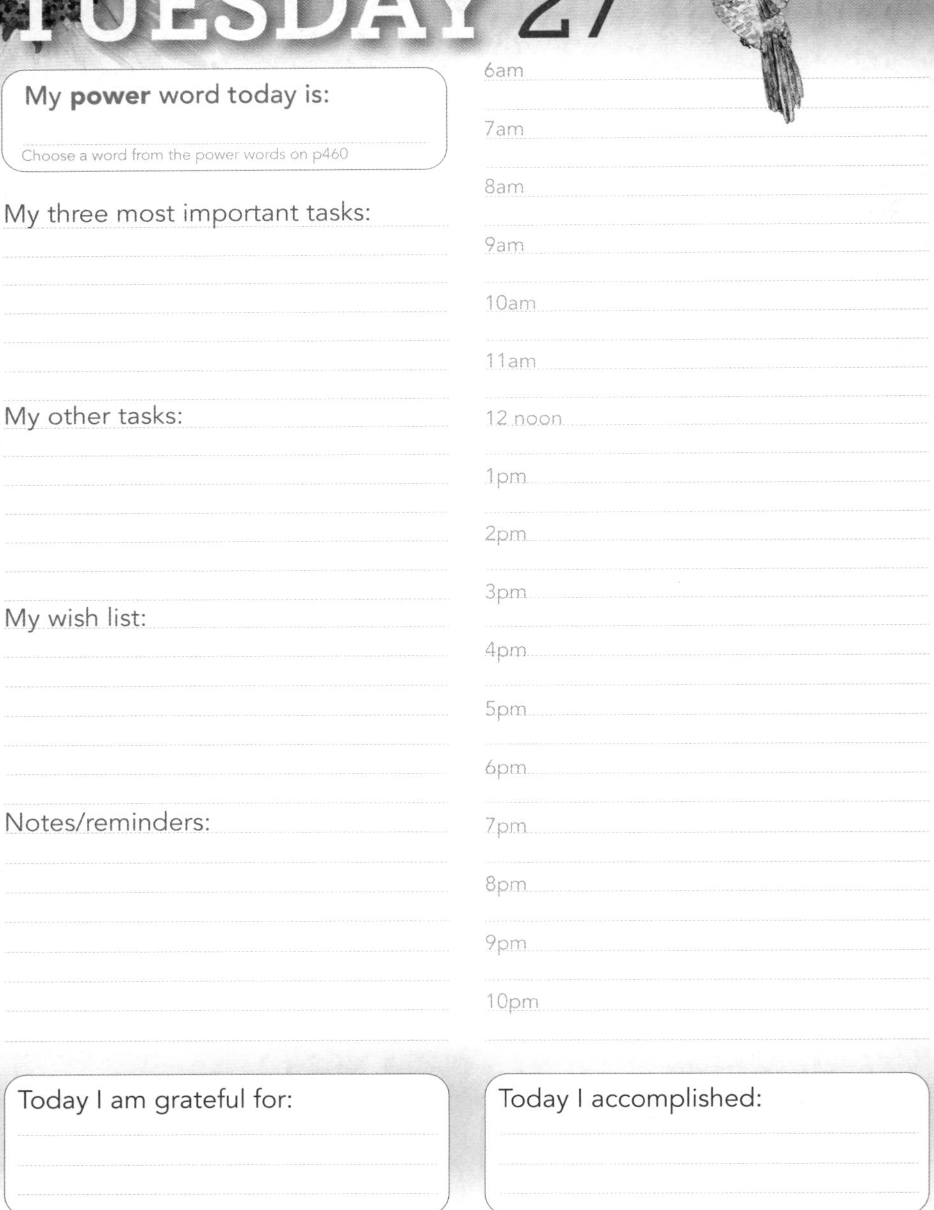

My **power** word today is:

Choose a word from the power words on p460

My three most important tasks:

My other tasks:

My wish list:

Notes/reminders:

6am

7am

8am

9am

10am

11am

12 noon

1pm

2pm

3pm

4pm

5pm

6pm

7pm

8pm

9pm

10pm

Today I am grateful for:

Today I accomplished:

Don't curse the dark – light a candle.

JULY

WEDNESDAY 28

My **power** word today is:

Choose a word from the power words on p460

My three most important tasks:

My other tasks:

My wish list:

Notes/reminders:

6am

7am

8am

9am

10am

11am

12 noon

1pm

2pm

3pm

4pm

5pm

6pm

7pm

8pm

9pm

10pm

Today I am grateful for:

Today I accomplished:

What doesn't kill you makes you stronger.

JULY

THURSDAY 29

My **power** word today is:

Choose a word from the power words on p460

My three most important tasks:

My other tasks:

My wish list:

Notes/reminders:

6am

7am

8am

9am

10am

11am

12 noon

1pm

2pm

3pm

4pm

5pm

6pm

7pm

8pm

9pm

10pm

Today I am grateful for:

Today I accomplished:

Personally, I try to take nothing personally.

JULY

FRIDAY 30

My **power** word today is:

Choose a word from the power words on p460

My three most important tasks:

My other tasks:

My wish list:

Notes/reminders:

6am

7am

8am

9am

10am

11am

12 noon

1pm

2pm

3pm

4pm

5pm

6pm

7pm

8pm

9pm

10pm

Today I am grateful for:

Today I accomplished:

Look for advice when you need it – and take it!

JULY

SATURDAY 31

My **power** word today is:

Choose a word from the power words on p460

My three most important tasks:

My other tasks:

My wish list:

Notes/reminders:

6am

7am

8am

9am

10am

11am

12 noon

1pm

2pm

3pm

4pm

5pm

6pm

7pm

8pm

9pm

10pm

Today I am grateful for:

Today I accomplished:

A helping hand is better than a load of advice.

JULY

Monthly reflections

It may be that those who do most, dream most.
Stephen Butler Leacock

Best moments:

Greatest accomplishments:

Toughest challenge:

Biggest learnings:

Progress towards ongoing goals:

Remember your 2021 promises and your BIG WHY.
Remind yourself of your motives on page 10.

MY TOP FIVES

MY TOP FIVE PASSIONS

1
2
3
4
5

MY TOP FIVE TALENTS

1
2
3
4
5

MY TOP FIVE ROLE MODELS

1
2
3
4
5

MY TOP FIVE VALUES

1
2
3
4
5

MY TOP FIVE GOALS

1
2
3
4
5

AUGUST

Nurture your mind with great thoughts, for you will never go any higher than you think.

Benjamin Disraeli

AUGUST

AT A GLANCE

MONDAY	TUESDAY	WEDNESDAY	THURSDAY	FRIDAY	SATURDAY	SUNDAY
						1
2	3	4	5	6	7	8
9	10	11	12	13	14	15
16	17	18	19	20	21	22
23	24	25	26	27	28	29
30	31					

AUGUST ACTION PLANNER

A goal is a dream with a deadline

Dates/days to celebrate:

Events to attend:

People to meet/follow up:

Appointments to keep:

Trips to plan:

Purchases/payments to make:

Friends/family to contact:

Movies to see/books to read:

AUGUST

Monthly motivator

PRIORITIES

GOALS

CHALLENGES

ACTIONS

AUGUST

Financial tracker

MONTHLY CASH FLOW

	Personal	Business	Total
Income			
Salary			
Business dividend			
Pension			
Subsidy			
Other			
Total			
Living expenses			
Mortgage/rent			
Utilities/bills			
Credit card payments			
Loan repayments			
Insurance (home/car/life/health)			
Tax (personal/car/property)			
Savings			
Pension/investments			
House/garden			
Travel/fuel			
Groceries/toiletries			
Entertainment/dining out			
Education/training			
Child care			
Home care			
Health/self care/gym			
Other			
Total			
Total income			
Total outgoings			
Surplus/deficit			
This month's priority			

AUGUST

Food planner

Our bodies are our gardens –
our wills are our gardeners.

MY MENU PLANNER (grocery list)

Week 1

Week 2

Week 3

Week 4

Reflections and comments:

This month's meal ideas:

To keep the body in good health is a duty. Otherwise we shall not be able to keep our mind strong and clear.

MY HEALTHY NUTRITION PLAN

	BREAKFAST	LUNCH	DINNER	SNACKS	FRUIT	VEGETABLES	WATER
Week 1							
Week 2							
Week 3							
Week 4							

Reflections and comments:

This month's healthy eating ideas:

AUGUST

Health planner

After dinner rest a while;
after supper walk a mile.

MY EXERCISE PLAN

	ACTIVITY	DURATION	HR	WT/BMI	NOTES
Week 1					
Week 2					
Week 3					
Week 4					

Reflections and comments:

This month's fitness goal:

Adapt the remedy to the disease.

MY WELLBEING PLAN

	PHYSICAL	MENTAL/EMOTIONAL	SOCIAL	FINANCIAL
Week 1				
Week 2				
Week 3				
Week 4				

Reflections and comments:

This month's wellbeing goal:

AUGUST

Doodles and ideas

5 TIPS FOR MINDFULNESS

- Be aware of your surroundings
- Notice the little things
- Slow down
- Pay attention to what you are doing
- Contemplate where you are

AUGUST

SUNDAY 1

My **power** word today is:

Choose a word from the power words on p460

My three most important tasks:

My other tasks:

My wish list:

Notes/reminders:

6am

7am

8am

9am

10am

11am

12 noon

1pm

2pm

3pm

4pm

5pm

6pm

7pm

8pm

9pm

10pm

Today I am grateful for:

Today I accomplished:

You are not alone.

AUGUST • Bank Holiday

MONDAY 2

This week's focus:

My **power** word today is:

Choose a word from the power words on p460

My three most important tasks:

My other tasks:

My wish list:

Notes/reminders:

6am

7am

8am

9am

10am

11am

12 noon

1pm

2pm

3pm

4pm

5pm

6pm

7pm

8pm

9pm

10pm

Today I am grateful for:

Today I accomplished:

There is only now and it's happening now.

AUGUST

TUESDAY 3

My **power** word today is:

Choose a word from the power words on p460

My three most important tasks:

My other tasks:

My wish list:

Notes/reminders:

6am

7am

8am

9am

10am

11am

12 noon

1pm

2pm

3pm

4pm

5pm

6pm

7pm

8pm

9pm

10pm

Today I am grateful for:

Today I accomplished:

Dream more while you are awake.

AUGUST

WEDNESDAY 4

My **power** word today is:

Choose a word from the power words on p460

My three most important tasks:

My other tasks:

My wish list:

Notes/reminders:

6am

7am

8am

9am

10am

11am

12 noon

1pm

2pm

3pm

4pm

5pm

6pm

7pm

8pm

9pm

10pm

Today I am grateful for:

Today I accomplished:

Keep moving – don't be hesitant or afraid.

AUGUST

THURSDAY 5

My **power** word today is:

Choose a word from the power words on p460

My three most important tasks:

My other tasks:

My wish list:

Notes/reminders:

6am

7am

8am

9am

10am

11am

12 noon

1pm

2pm

3pm

4pm

5pm

6pm

7pm

8pm

9pm

10pm

Today I am grateful for:

Today I accomplished:

Make peace with your past to have peace in your future.

AUGUST

FRIDAY 6

My **power** word today is:

Choose a word from the power words on p460

My three most important tasks:

My other tasks:

My wish list:

Notes/reminders:

6am

7am

8am

9am

10am

11am

12 noon

1pm

2pm

3pm

4pm

5pm

6pm

7pm

8pm

9pm

10pm

Today I am grateful for:

Today I accomplished:

The most wasted of all days is the one without a smile.

SATURDAY 7

My **power** word today is:

Choose a word from the power words on p460

SUNDAY 8

My **power** word today is:

Choose a word from the power words on p460

Stop trying to please everyone.

AUGUST

MONDAY 9

This week's focus:

My **power** word today is:

Choose a word from the power words on p460

My three most important tasks:

My other tasks:

My wish list:

Notes/reminders:

6am

7am

8am

9am

10am

11am

12 noon

1pm

2pm

3pm

4pm

5pm

6pm

7pm

8pm

9pm

10pm

Today I am grateful for:

Today I accomplished:

Resist buying something you don't need.

AUGUST

TUESDAY 10

My **power** word today is:

Choose a word from the power words on p460

My three most important tasks:

My other tasks:

My wish list:

Notes/reminders:

6am

7am

8am

9am

10am

11am

12 noon

1pm

2pm

3pm

4pm

5pm

6pm

7pm

8pm

9pm

10pm

Today I am grateful for:

Today I accomplished:

Focus on a future that ignites your enthusiasm in the present.

AUGUST

WEDNESDAY 11

My **power** word today is:

Choose a word from the power words on p460

My three most important tasks:

My other tasks:

My wish list:

Notes/reminders:

6am

7am

8am

9am

10am

11am

12 noon

1pm

2pm

3pm

4pm

5pm

6pm

7pm

8pm

9pm

10pm

Today I am grateful for:

Today I accomplished:

Do not give up while you still have something to give.

AUGUST

THURSDAY 12

My **power** word today is:

Choose a word from the power words on p460

My three most important tasks:

My other tasks:

My wish list:

Notes/reminders:

6am

7am

8am

9am

10am

11am

12 noon

1pm

2pm

3pm

4pm

5pm

6pm

7pm

8pm

9pm

10pm

Today I am grateful for:

Today I accomplished:

Do as you would be done by.

AUGUST

FRIDAY 13

My **power** word today is:

Choose a word from the power words on p460

My three most important tasks:

My other tasks:

My wish list:

Notes/reminders:

6am

7am

8am

9am

10am

11am

12 noon

1pm

2pm

3pm

4pm

5pm

6pm

7pm

8pm

9pm

10pm

Today I am grateful for:

Today I accomplished:

Prepare to live an awesome life.

AUGUST

SATURDAY 14

My **power** word today is:

Choose a word from the power words on p460

SUNDAY 15

My **power** word today is:

Choose a word from the power words on p460

Take pleasure in simple pleasures.

AUGUST

MONDAY 16

This week's focus:

My **power** word today is:

Choose a word from the power words on p460

My three most important tasks:

My other tasks:

My wish list:

Notes/reminders:

6am

7am

8am

9am

10am

11am

12 noon

1pm

2pm

3pm

4pm

5pm

6pm

7pm

8pm

9pm

10pm

Today I am grateful for:

Today I accomplished:

It's by taking chances that we learn to be brave.

AUGUST

TUESDAY 17

My **power** word today is:

Choose a word from the power words on p460

on p460

My three most important tasks:

My other tasks:

My wish list:

Notes/reminders:

6am

7am

8am

9am

10am

11am

12 noon

1pm

2pm

3pm

4pm

5pm

6pm

7pm

8pm

9pm

10pm

Today I am grateful for:

Today I accomplished:

Set big goals but keep tasks small.

AUGUST

WEDNESDAY 18

My **power** word today is:

Choose a word from the power words on p460

My three most important tasks:

My other tasks:

My wish list:

Notes/reminders:

6am

7am

8am

9am

10am

11am

12 noon

1pm

2pm

3pm

4pm

5pm

6pm

7pm

8pm

9pm

10pm

Today I am grateful for:

Today I accomplished:

Don't undermine your worth by comparing yourself to others.

AUGUST

THURSDAY 19

My **power** word today is:

Choose a word from the power words on p460

Choose a word from the power words on p460

My three most important tasks:

My other tasks:

My wish list:

Notes/reminders:

6am

7am

8am

9am

10am

11am

12 noon

1pm

2pm

3pm

4pm

5pm

6pm

7pm

8pm

9pm

10pm

Today I am grateful for:

Today I accomplished:

What ever you do, do it well.

AUGUST

FRIDAY 20

My **power** word today is:

Choose a word from the power words on p460

My three most important tasks:

My other tasks:

My wish list:

Notes/reminders:

6am

7am

8am

9am

10am

11am

12 noon

1pm

2pm

3pm

4pm

5pm

6pm

7pm

8pm

9pm

10pm

Today I am grateful for:

Today I accomplished:

Your life can be what you want it to be.

AUGUST

SATURDAY 21

My **power** word today is:

Choose a word from the power words on p460

SUNDAY 22

My **power** word today is:

Choose a word from the power words on p460

You get from people what you expect.

AUGUST

MONDAY 23

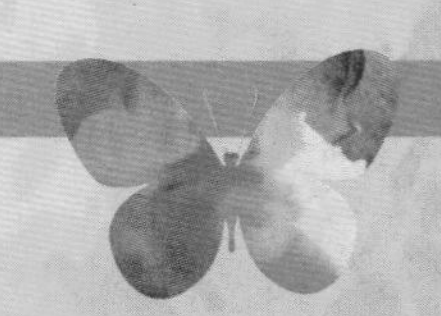

This week's focus:

My **power** word today is:

Choose a word from the power words on p460

My three most important tasks:

My other tasks:

My wish list:

Notes/reminders:

6am

7am

8am

9am

10am

11am

12 noon

1pm

2pm

3pm

4pm

5pm

6pm

7pm

8pm

9pm

10pm

Today I am grateful for:

Today I accomplished:

Pay attention to the flow of life.

AUGUST

TUESDAY 24

My **power** word today is:

Choose a word from the power words on p460

My three most important tasks:

My other tasks:

My wish list:

Notes/reminders:

6am

7am

8am

9am

10am

11am

12 noon

1pm

2pm

3pm

4pm

5pm

6pm

7pm

8pm

9pm

10pm

Today I am grateful for:

Today I accomplished:

Make time for silence.

AUGUST

WEDNESDAY 25

My **power** word today is:

Choose a word from the power words on p460

My three most important tasks:

My other tasks:

My wish list:

Notes/reminders:

6am

7am

8am

9am

10am

11am

12 noon

1pm

2pm

3pm

4pm

5pm

6pm

7pm

8pm

9pm

10pm

Today I am grateful for:

Today I accomplished:

Use your passion to inspire your purpose.

AUGUST

THURSDAY 26

My **power** word today is:

Choose a word from the power words on p460

My three most important tasks:

My other tasks:

My wish list:

Notes/reminders:

6am

7am

8am

9am

10am

11am

12 noon

1pm

2pm

3pm

4pm

5pm

6pm

7pm

8pm

9pm

10pm

Today I am grateful for:

Today I accomplished:

Leave space in your life for spontaneous happenings.

AUGUST

FRIDAY 27

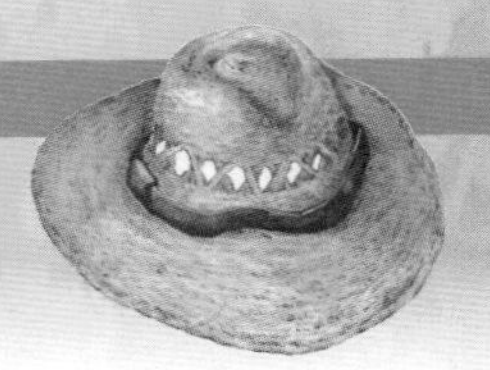

My **power** word today is:

Choose a word from the power words on p460

My three most important tasks:

My other tasks:

My wish list:

Notes/reminders:

6am

7am

8am

9am

10am

11am

12 noon

1pm

2pm

3pm

4pm

5pm

6pm

7pm

8pm

9pm

10pm

Today I am grateful for:

Today I accomplished:

Don't look back, you'll miss what's in front of you.

SATURDAY 28

My **power** word today is:

Choose a word from the power words on p460

SUNDAY 29

My **power** word today is:

Choose a word from the power words on p460

What you do now matters.

AUGUST

MONDAY 30

This week's focus:

My **power** word today is:

Choose a word from the power words on p460

My three most important tasks:

My other tasks:

My wish list:

Notes/reminders:

6am

7am

8am

9am

10am

11am

12 noon

1pm

2pm

3pm

4pm

5pm

6pm

7pm

8pm

9pm

10pm

Today I am grateful for:

Today I accomplished:

Act consistent with your values.

AUGUST

TUESDAY 31

My **power** word today is:

Choose a word from the power words on p460

My three most important tasks:

My other tasks:

My wish list:

Notes/reminders:

6am

7am

8am

9am

10am

11am

12 noon

1pm

2pm

3pm

4pm

5pm

6pm

7pm

8pm

9pm

10pm

Today I am grateful for:

Today I accomplished:

There is a reason for everything.

AUGUST

Monthly reflections

If one advances confidently in the direction of one's dreams, and endeavors to live the life which one has imagined, one will meet with a success unexpected in common hours.

Henry David Thoreau

Best moments:

Greatest accomplishments:

Toughest challenge:

Biggest learnings:

Progress towards ongoing goals:

Remember your 2021 promises and your BIG WHY.
Remind yourself of your motives on page 10.

SEPTEMBER

Cherish your visions and your dreams as they are the children of your soul, the blueprints of your ultimate achievements.

Napoleon Hill

SEPTEMBER

AT A GLANCE

MONDAY	TUESDAY	WEDNESDAY	THURSDAY	FRIDAY	SATURDAY	SUNDAY
		1	2	3	4	5
6	7	8	9	10	11	12
13	14	15	16	17	18	19
20	21	22	23	24	25	26
27	28	29	30			

SEPTEMBER ACTION PLANNER

A goal is a dream with a deadline

Dates/days to celebrate:

Events to attend:

People to meet/follow up:

Appointments to keep:

Trips to plan:

Purchases/payments to make:

Friends/family to contact:

Movies to see/books to read:

SEPTEMBER

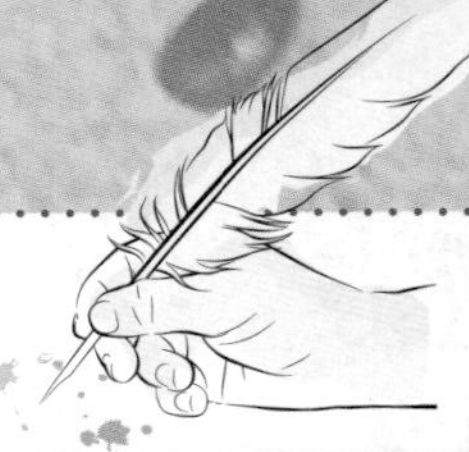

Monthly motivator

PRIORITIES

GOALS

CHALLENGES

ACTIONS

SEPTEMBER

Financial tracker

MONTHLY CASH FLOW

	Personal	Business	Total
Income			
Salary			
Business dividend			
Pension			
Subsidy			
Other			
Total			
Living expenses			
Mortgage/rent			
Utilities/bills			
Credit card payments			
Loan repayments			
Insurance (home/car/life/health)			
Tax (personal/car/property)			
Savings			
Pension/investments			
House/garden			
Travel/fuel			
Groceries/toiletries			
Entertainment/dining out			
Education/training			
Child care			
Home care			
Health/self care/gym			
Other			
Total			
Total income			
Total outgoings			
Surplus/deficit			
This month's priority			

SEPTEMBER

Food planner

If you keep good food in your fridge, you will eat good food.

MY MENU PLANNER (grocery list)

Week 1

Week 2

Week 3

Week 4

Reflections and comments:

This month's meal ideas:

The more you eat, the less flavour; the less you eat, the more flavour.
Chinese proverb

MY HEALTHY NUTRITION PLAN

	BREAKFAST	LUNCH	DINNER	SNACKS	FRUIT	VEGETABLES	WATER
Week 1							
Week 2							
Week 3							
Week 4							

Reflections and comments:

This month's healthy eating ideas:

SEPTEMBER

Health planner

The preservation of health is a duty.

MY EXERCISE PLAN

	ACTIVITY	DURATION	HR	WT/BMI	NOTES
Week 1					
Week 2					
Week 3					
Week 4					

Reflections and comments:

This month's fitness goal:

Be careful about reading healthbooks. You may die of a misprint.
Mark Twain

MY WELLBEING PLAN

	PHYSICAL	MENTAL/EMOTIONAL	SOCIAL	FINANCIAL
Week 1				
Week 2				
Week 3				
Week 4				

Reflections and comments:

This month's wellbeing goal:

SEPTEMBER

Doodles and ideas

5 TIPS FOR PERSONAL GROWTH

- Develop a learning mindset
- Be willing to challenge your status quo
- Have inspiring role models
- Be courageous in pursuit of your goals
- Play a big game

REST *and* RELAXATION

Check up for mental and physical wellbeing.

	CURRENT HOURS PER WEEK	DESIRED HOURS PER WEEK
Self care		
Sleep		
Meditation		
Yoga		
Massage		
Journaling		
Social media		
TV		
Movies		
Reading		
Exercise		
Leisure walking		
Creative writing		
Pets		
Outdoor pursuits		

	CURRENT HOURS PER WEEK	DESIRED HOURS PER WEEK
Indoor games		
Sports		
Family fun		
Art		
Conversation		
Music		
Dance		
Theatre		
Eating out		
Visiting friends		
Entertaining at home		
Partying		
Holidays		
Weekend away		

AFTER A WHILE YOU LEARN

After a while you learn
The subtle difference between
Holding a hand and chaining a soul.
And you learn that love doesn't mean leaning,
And company doesn't always mean security.
And you begin to learn
That kisses aren't contracts
And presents aren't promises.
And you begin to accept your defeats
With the grace of a woman,
Not the grief of a child.
And you learn
To build all your roads on today,
Because tomorrow's ground is
Too uncertain for plans.
And futures have a way of falling down in mid-flight.
After a while you learn
That even sunshine burns if you get too much.
So you plant your own garden
And decorate your own soul
Instead of waiting for someone
To bring you flowers.
And you learn
That you really can endure,
That you really are strong,
And you really do have worth.
And you learn and you learn.
With every goodbye you learn.

Veronica A Shoffstall

SEPTEMBER

WEDNESDAY 1

My **power** word today is:

Choose a word from the power words on p460

My three most important tasks:

My other tasks:

My wish list:

Notes/reminders:

6am

7am

8am

9am

10am

11am

12 noon

1pm

2pm

3pm

4pm

5pm

6pm

7pm

8pm

9pm

10pm

Today I am grateful for:

Today I accomplished:

Live your life with passion and purpose.

SEPTEMBER

THURSDAY 2

My **power** word today is:

Choose a word from the power words on p460

My three most important tasks:

My other tasks:

My wish list:

Notes/reminders:

6am

7am

8am

9am

10am

11am

12 noon

1pm

2pm

3pm

4pm

5pm

6pm

7pm

8pm

9pm

10pm

Today I am grateful for:

Today I accomplished:

Compose a mission statement for your life.

SEPTEMBER

FRIDAY 3

My **power** word today is:

Choose a word from the power words on p460

My three most important tasks:

My other tasks:

My wish list:

Notes/reminders:

6am

7am

8am

9am

10am

11am

12 noon

1pm

2pm

3pm

4pm

5pm

6pm

7pm

8pm

9pm

10pm

Today I am grateful for:

Today I accomplished:

Let your light shine.

SATURDAY 4

My **power** word today is:

Choose a word from the power words on p460

SUNDAY 5

My **power** word today is:

Choose a word from the power words on p460

Courage and confidence come from within.

SEPTEMBER

MONDAY 6

This week's focus:

My **power** word today is:

Choose a word from the power words on p460

My three most important tasks:

My other tasks:

My wish list:

Notes/reminders:

6am

7am

8am

9am

10am

11am

12 noon

1pm

2pm

3pm

4pm

5pm

6pm

7pm

8pm

9pm

10pm

Today I am grateful for:

Today I accomplished:

See beauty in unexpected places.

TUESDAY 7

My **power** word today is:

Choose a word from the power words on p460

My three most important tasks:

My other tasks:

My wish list:

Notes/reminders:

6am

7am

8am

9am

10am

11am

12 noon

1pm

2pm

3pm

4pm

5pm

6pm

7pm

8pm

9pm

10pm

Today I am grateful for:

Today I accomplished:

Be master of your habits or they will master you.

SEPTEMBER

WEDNESDAY 8

My **power** word today is:

Choose a word from the power words on p460

My three most important tasks:

My other tasks:

My wish list:

Notes/reminders:

6am

7am

8am

9am

10am

11am

12 noon

1pm

2pm

3pm

4pm

5pm

6pm

7pm

8pm

9pm

10pm

Today I am grateful for:

Today I accomplished:

Begin where you are now.

THURSDAY 9

My **power** word today is:

Choose a word from the power words on p460

My three most important tasks:

My other tasks:

My wish list:

Notes/reminders:

6am

7am

8am

9am

10am

11am

12 noon

1pm

2pm

3pm

4pm

5pm

6pm

7pm

8pm

9pm

10pm

Today I am grateful for:

Today I accomplished:

Be open to the contribution of others.

SEPTEMBER

FRIDAY 10

My **power** word today is:

Choose a word from the power words on p460

My three most important tasks:

My other tasks:

My wish list:

Notes/reminders:

6am

7am

8am

9am

10am

11am

12 noon

1pm

2pm

3pm

4pm

5pm

6pm

7pm

8pm

9pm

10pm

Today I am grateful for:

Today I accomplished:

Make your own luck.

SEPTEMBER

SATURDAY 11

My **power** word today is:

Choose a word from the power words on p460

SUNDAY 12

My **power** word today is:

Choose a word from the power words on p460

Take the initiative.

SEPTEMBER

MONDAY 13

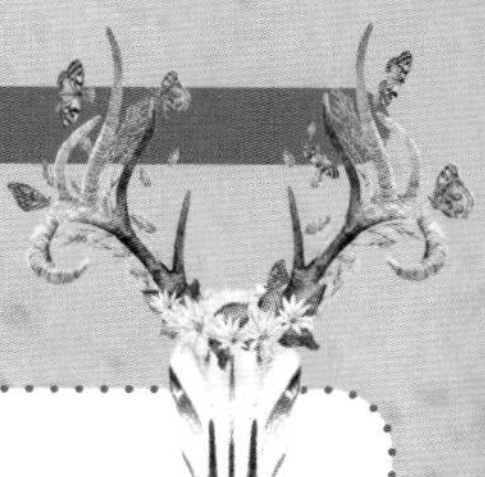

This week's focus:

My **power** word today is:

Choose a word from the power words on p460

My three most important tasks:

My other tasks:

My wish list:

Notes/reminders:

6am

7am

8am

9am

10am

11am

12 noon

1pm

2pm

3pm

4pm

5pm

6pm

7pm

8pm

9pm

10pm

Today I am grateful for:

Today I accomplished:

Everyone thinks differently.

SEPTEMBER

TUESDAY 14

My power word today is:

Choose a word from the power words on p460

My three most important tasks:

My other tasks:

My wish list:

Notes/reminders:

6am

7am

8am

9am

10am

11am

12 noon

1pm

2pm

3pm

4pm

5pm

6pm

7pm

8pm

9pm

10pm

Today I am grateful for:

Today I accomplished:

Don't complain about what you permit.

SEPTEMBER

WEDNESDAY 15

My power word today is:

Choose a word from the power words on p460

My three most important tasks:

My other tasks:

My wish list:

Notes/reminders:

6am

7am

8am

9am

10am

11am

12 noon

1pm

2pm

3pm

4pm

5pm

6pm

7pm

8pm

9pm

10pm

Today I am grateful for:

Today I accomplished:

Do one thing at a time.

SEPTEMBER

THURSDAY 16

My **power** word today is:

Choose a word from the power words on p460

My three most important tasks:

My other tasks:

My wish list:

Notes/reminders:

6am

7am

8am

9am

10am

11am

12 noon

1pm

2pm

3pm

4pm

5pm

6pm

7pm

8pm

9pm

10pm

Today I am grateful for:

Today I accomplished:

Explore new possibilities.

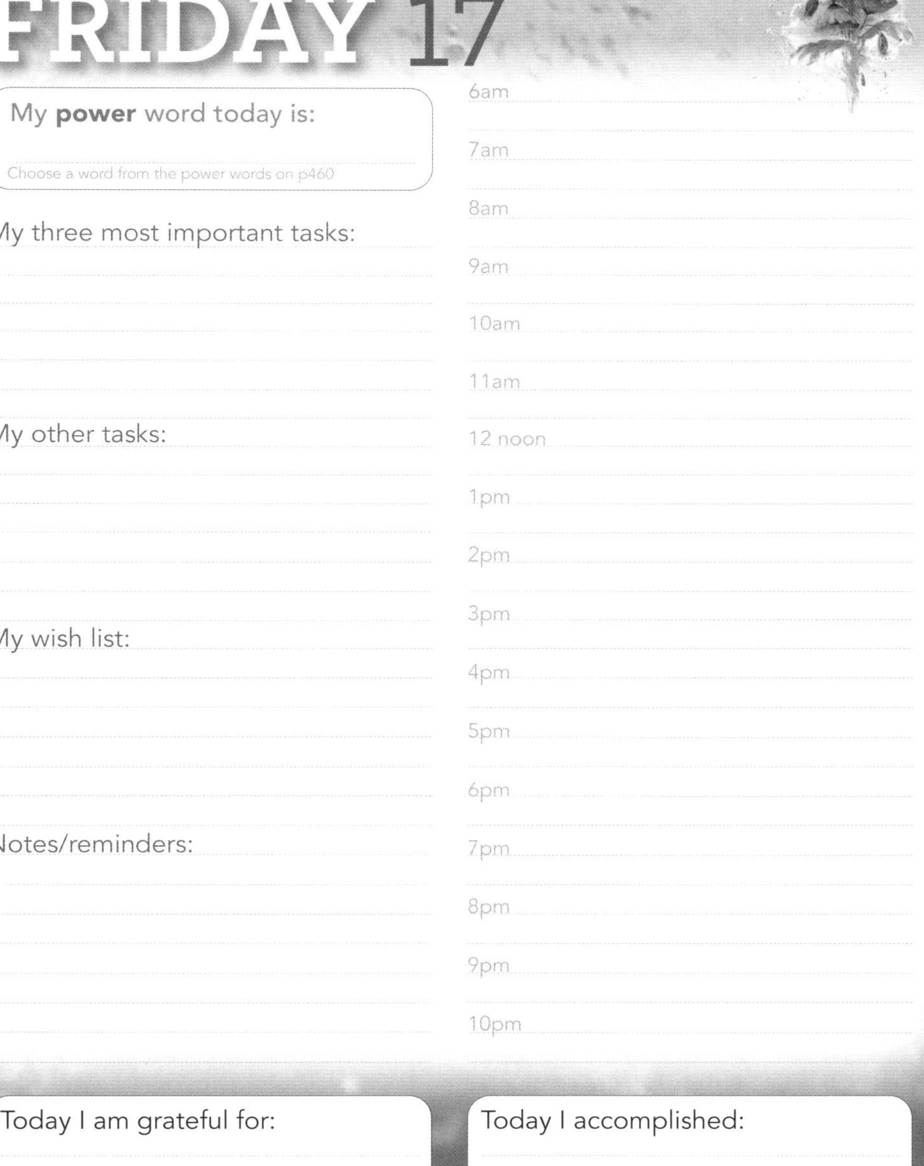

SEPTEMBER

FRIDAY 17

My **power** word today is:

Choose a word from the power words on p460

My three most important tasks:

My other tasks:

My wish list:

Notes/reminders:

6am

7am

8am

9am

10am

11am

12 noon

1pm

2pm

3pm

4pm

5pm

6pm

7pm

8pm

9pm

10pm

Today I am grateful for:

Today I accomplished:

Nothing wastes more time than worrying.

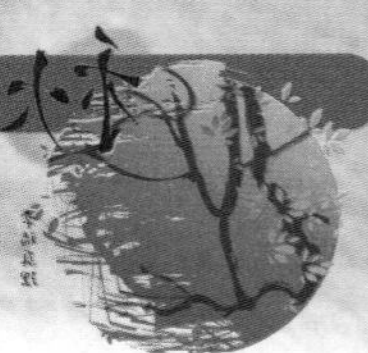

SATURDAY 18

My **power** word today is:

Choose a word from the power words on p460

SUNDAY 19

My **power** word today is:

Choose a word from the power words on p460

Improvement begins with 'I'.

SEPTEMBER

MONDAY 20

This week's focus:

My **power** word today is:

Choose a word from the power words on p460

My three most important tasks:

My other tasks:

My wish list:

Notes/reminders:

6am

7am

8am

9am

10am

11am

12 noon

1pm

2pm

3pm

4pm

5pm

6pm

7pm

8pm

9pm

10pm

Today I am grateful for:

Today I accomplished:

Nothing ventured noting gained.

SEPTEMBER

TUESDAY 21

My **power** word today is:

Choose a word from the power words on p460

My three most important tasks:

My other tasks:

My wish list:

Notes/reminders:

6am

7am

8am

9am

10am

11am

12 noon

1pm

2pm

3pm

4pm

5pm

6pm

7pm

8pm

9pm

10pm

Today I am grateful for:

Today I accomplished:

Schedule some time to do something you have never done before.

SEPTEMBER

WEDNESDAY 22

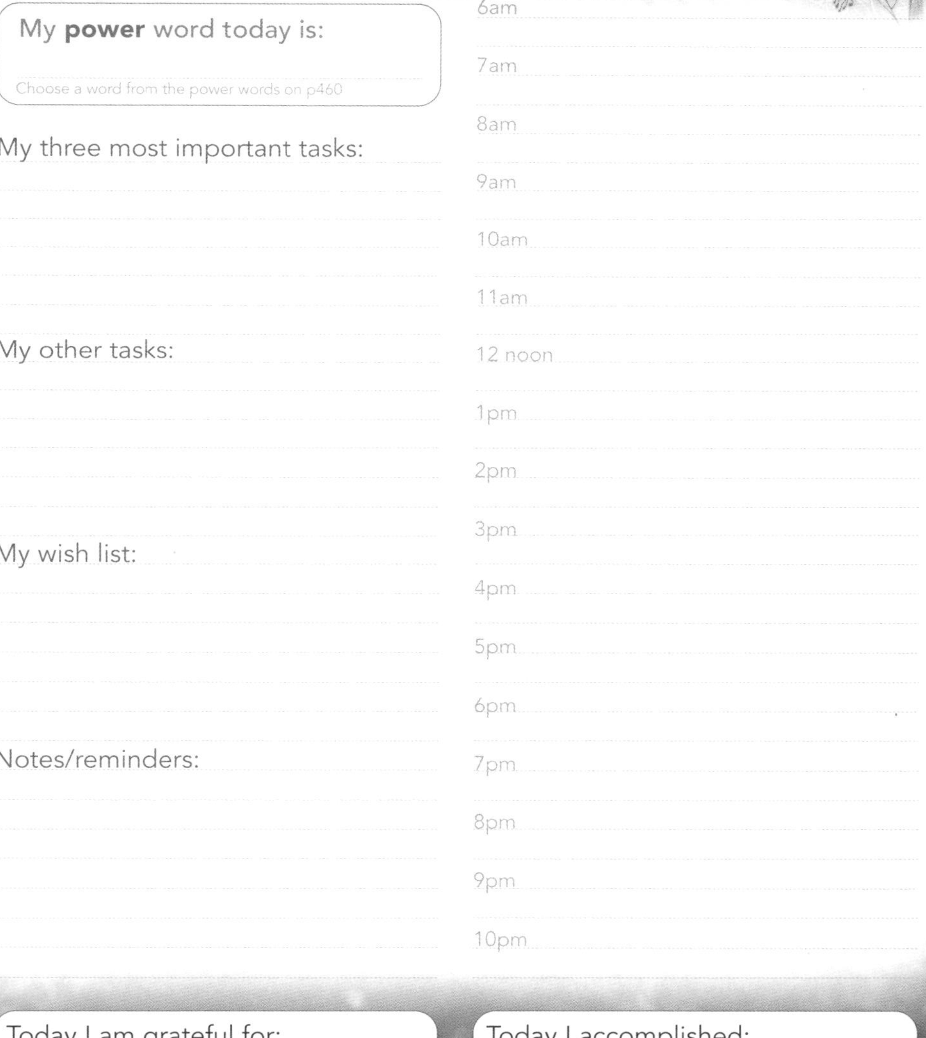

Today I am grateful for:

Today I accomplished:

There is no 'no' in life.

SEPTEMBER

THURSDAY 23

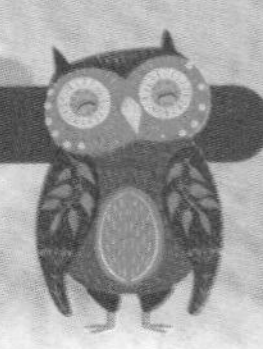

My **power** word today is:

Choose a word from the power words on p460

My three most important tasks:

My other tasks:

My wish list:

Notes/reminders:

6am

7am

8am

9am

10am

11am

12 noon

1pm

2pm

3pm

4pm

5pm

6pm

7pm

8pm

9pm

10pm

Today I am grateful for:

Today I accomplished:

Your mind matters, mind it.

SEPTEMBER

My **power** word today is:

Choose a word from the power words on p460

My three most important tasks:

My other tasks:

My wish list:

Notes/reminders:

6am

7am

8am

9am

10am

11am

12 noon

1pm

2pm

3pm

4pm

5pm

6pm

7pm

8pm

9pm

10pm

Today I am grateful for:

Today I accomplished:

Aim to be at the source of your life, not the effect.

SATURDAY 25

My **power** word today is:

Choose a word from the power words on p460

SUNDAY 26

My **power** word today is:

Choose a word from the power words on p460

Be kind to everyone – including yourself.

SEPTEMBER

MONDAY 27

This week's focus:

My **power** word today is:

Choose a word from the power words on p460

My three most important tasks:

My other tasks:

My wish list:

Notes/reminders:

6am

7am

8am

9am

10am

11am

12 noon

1pm

2pm

3pm

4pm

5pm

6pm

7pm

8pm

9pm

10pm

Today I am grateful for:

Today I accomplished:

Don't be afraid to look bad for a good cause.

SEPTEMBER

TUESDAY 28

My **power** word today is:

Choose a word from the power words on p460

My three most important tasks:

My other tasks:

My wish list:

Notes/reminders:

6am

7am

8am

9am

10am

11am

12 noon

1pm

2pm

3pm

4pm

5pm

6pm

7pm

8pm

9pm

10pm

Today I am grateful for:

Today I accomplished:

Don't hold grudges.

SEPTEMBER

WEDNESDAY 29

My **power** word today is:

Choose a word from the power words on p460

My three most important tasks:

My other tasks:

My wish list:

Notes/reminders:

6am

7am

8am

9am

10am

11am

12 noon

1pm

2pm

3pm

4pm

5pm

6pm

7pm

8pm

9pm

10pm

Today I am grateful for:

Today I accomplished:

Don't believe everything you hear.

SEPTEMBER

THURSDAY 30

My **power** word today is:

Choose a word from the power words on p460

My three most important tasks:

My other tasks:

My wish list:

Notes/reminders:

6am

7am

8am

9am

10am

11am

12 noon

1pm

2pm

3pm

4pm

5pm

6pm

7pm

8pm

9pm

10pm

Today I am grateful for:

Today I accomplished:

Follow your heart.

SEPTEMBER

Monthly reflections

Never give up on a dream just because of the time it will take to accomplish it. The time will pass anyway.
Earl Nightingale

Best moments:

Greatest accomplishments:

Toughest challenge:

Biggest learnings:

Progress towards ongoing goals:

Remember your 2021 promises and your BIG WHY.
Remind yourself of your motives on page 10.

Quarterly check-in

YES	NO	
☐	☐	Are you eating in a way that supports your good health?
☐	☐	Are you getting enough sleep?
☐	☐	Are you participating in regular physical exercise?
☐	☐	Are you managing your finances?
☐	☐	Are you enjoying your work/career?
☐	☐	Are you caring for yourself responsibly?
☐	☐	Are you engaged with your community?
☐	☐	Are you meeting friends and family frequently?
☐	☐	Are you journaling/painting/writing/dancing/ singing?
☐	☐	Is your house/car/office/desk tidy?
☐	☐	Is your communication clear and straight?
☐	☐	Are you satisfied with how you are living your life?
☐	☐	Are you avoiding anything/anyone?
☐	☐	Are you ignoring/resisting anything?
☐	☐	Are you being a good role model in your life?
☐	☐	Are your relationships/partnerships thriving?
☐	☐	Are you growing in courage and confidence?
☐	☐	Are you taking on new challenges with interest?
☐	☐	Are you curious and excited about the future?
☐	☐	Are you working towards fulfilling your dreams?

Areas to work on/improve in the next three months:

OCTOBER

There is no cosmetic for beauty like happiness.

Lady Blessington

OCTOBER AT A GLANCE

MONDAY	TUESDAY	WEDNESDAY	THURSDAY	FRIDAY	SATURDAY	SUNDAY
				1	2	3
4	5	6	7	8	9	10
11	12	13	14	15	16	17
18	19	20	21	22	23	24
25	26	27	28	29	30	31

OCTOBER
ACTION PLANNER

A goal is a dream with a deadline

Dates/days to celebrate:

Events to attend:

People to meet/follow up:

Appointments to keep:

Trips to plan:

Purchases/payments to make:

Friends/family to contact:

Movies to see/books to read:

OCTOBER

Monthly motivator

PRIORITIES

GOALS

CHALLENGES

ACTIONS

OCTOBER

Financial tracker

MONTHLY CASH FLOW

	Personal	Business	Total
Income			
Salary			
Business dividend			
Pension			
Subsidy			
Other			
Total			
Living expenses			
Mortgage/rent			
Utilities/bills			
Credit card payments			
Loan repayments			
Insurance (home/car/life/health)			
Tax (personal/car/property)			
Savings			
Pension/investments			
House/garden			
Travel/fuel			
Groceries/toiletries			
Entertainment/dining out			
Education/training			
Child care			
Home care			
Health/self care/gym			
Other			
Total			
Total income			
Total outgoings			
Surplus/deficit			
This month's priority			

OCTOBER

Food planner

You are what you eat, so don't be fast, cheap, easy, or fake.

MY MENU PLANNER (grocery list)

Week 1

Week 2

Week 3

Week 4

Reflections and comments:

This month's meal ideas:

Your diet is a bank account. Good food choices are good investments.

MY HEALTHY NUTRITION PLAN

	BREAKFAST	LUNCH	DINNER	SNACKS	FRUIT	VEGETABLES	WATER
Week 1							
Week 2							
Week 3							
Week 4							

Reflections and comments:

This month's healthy eating ideas:

OCTOBER

Health planner

You don't get the ass you want by sitting on it.

MY EXERCISE PLAN

	ACTIVITY	DURATION	HR	WT/BMI	NOTES
Week 1					
Week 2					
Week 3					
Week 4					

Reflections and comments:

This month's fitness goal:

Few seem conscious that there is such a thing as physical morality.
Herbert Spencer

MY WELLBEING PLAN

	PHYSICAL	MENTAL/EMOTIONAL	SOCIAL	FINANCIAL
Week 1				
Week 2				
Week 3				
Week 4				

Reflections and comments:

This month's wellbeing goal:

OCTOBER

Doodles and ideas

5 TIPS FOR CREATIVITY

- Sing
- Paint
- Write
- Journal
- Dance

IMPORTANT SOFT SKILLS

Speaking skills: straight, clear, honest.
Listening skills: active, attentive, accepting.
People skills: relating, seeking common ground, acknowledgement.
Self awareness: aware of our attitudes, emotions, biases and beliefs.
Self management: nourishment, sleep, breaks.
Time management: schedule, calendar, clock.
Productivity: project focused, discipline, enjoy the task.
Leadership: visionary, inviting, supportive.
Team management: roles, responsibilities, trust.
Problem solving: creative, solution focused, outcome oriented.
Self mastery: mindful, reflective, responsible, resourceful.
Self expression: freedom, courage, confidence, contribution.

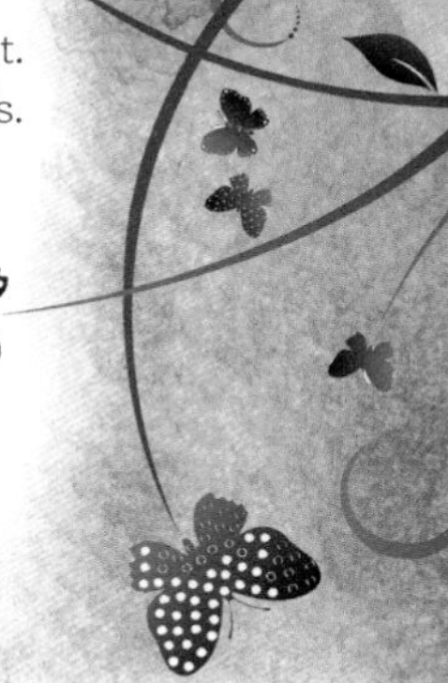

OUR GREATEST FEAR

Our deepest fear is not that we are inadequate.

Our deepest fear is that we are powerful beyond measure.
It is our light not our darkness that most frightens us.
We ask ourselves, who am I to be brilliant, gorgeous,
talented and fabulous?

Actually, who are you not to be?
You are a child of God.
Your playing small does not serve the world.
There's nothing enlightened about shrinking so that other
people won't feel insecure around you.

We were born to make manifest the glory of
God that is within us.

It's not just in some of us; it's in everyone.
And as we let our own light shine,
we unconsciously give other people
permission to do the same.
As we are liberated from our own fear,
Our presence automatically liberates others.

Marianne Williamson

OCTOBER

FRIDAY 1

My **power** word today is:

Choose a word from the power words on p460

My three most important tasks:

My other tasks:

My wish list:

Notes/reminders:

6am

7am

8am

9am

10am

11am

12 noon

1pm

2pm

3pm

4pm

5pm

6pm

7pm

8pm

9pm

10pm

Today I am grateful for:

Today I accomplished:

Focus on the positive, not the negative.

SATURDAY 2

My **power** word today is:

Choose a word from the power words on p460

SUNDAY 3

My **power** word today is:

Choose a word from the power words on p460

Always accept an apology.

OCTOBER

MONDAY 4

This week's focus:

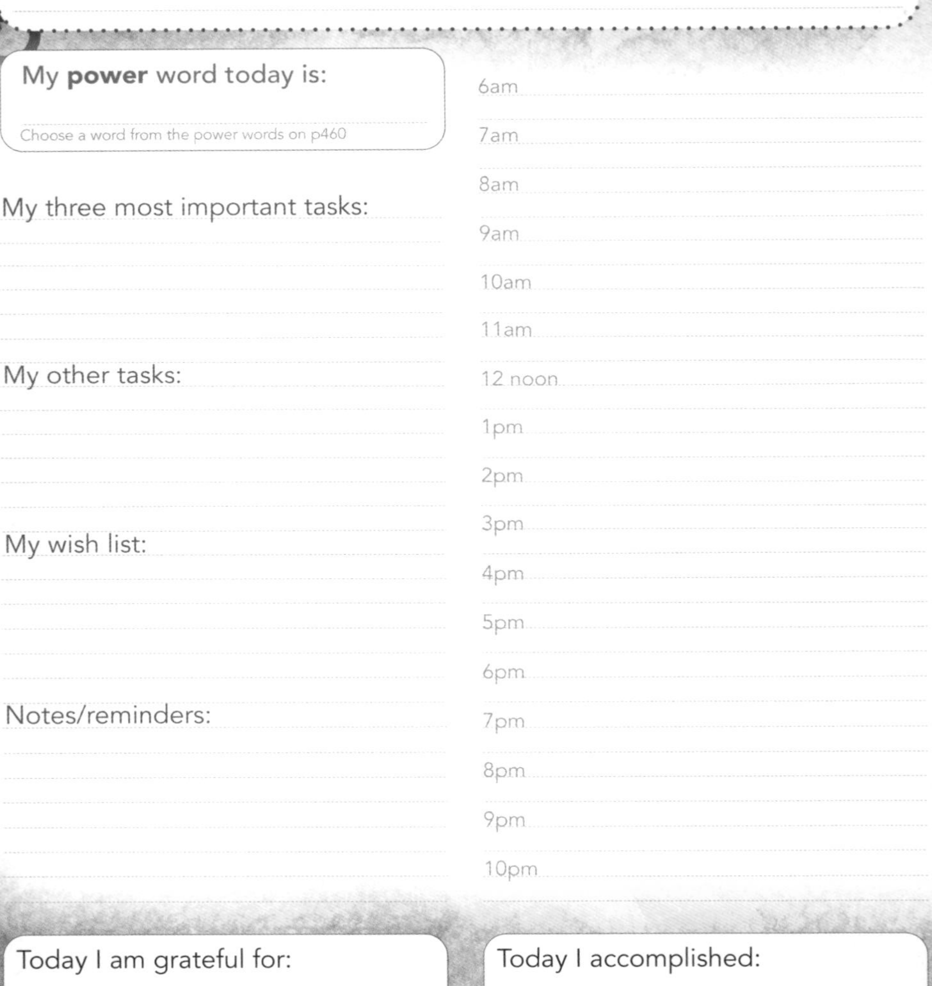

Today I am grateful for:

Today I accomplished:

Where there is trust, no proof is necessary.

OCTOBER

TUESDAY 5

My **power** word today is:

Choose a word from the power words on p460

My three most important tasks:

My other tasks:

My wish list:

Notes/reminders:

6am

7am

8am

9am

10am

11am

12 noon

1pm

2pm

3pm

4pm

5pm

6pm

7pm

8pm

9pm

10pm

Today I am grateful for:

Today I accomplished:

Life rewards decisive action.

OCTOBER

WEDNESDAY 6

My **power** word today is:

Choose a word from the power words on p460

My three most important tasks:

My other tasks:

My wish list:

Notes/reminders:

6am

7am

8am

9am

10am

11am

12 noon

1pm

2pm

3pm

4pm

5pm

6pm

7pm

8pm

9pm

10pm

Today I am grateful for:

Today I accomplished:

Procrastination is the thief of time.

OCTOBER

THURSDAY 7

My **power** word today is:

Choose a word from the power words on p460

My three most important tasks:

My other tasks:

My wish list:

Notes/reminders:

6am

7am

8am

9am

10am

11am

12 noon

1pm

2pm

3pm

4pm

5pm

6pm

7pm

8pm

9pm

10pm

Today I am grateful for:

Today I accomplished:

Be careful who's opinions you choose to agree with.

OCTOBER

FRIDAY 8

My **power** word today is:

Choose a word from the power words on p460

My three most important tasks:

My other tasks:

My wish list:

Notes/reminders:

6am

7am

8am

9am

10am

11am

12 noon

1pm

2pm

3pm

4pm

5pm

6pm

7pm

8pm

9pm

10pm

Today I am grateful for:

Today I accomplished:

Don't pretend in order to impress.

OCTOBER

SATURDAY 9

My **power** word today is:

Choose a word from the power words on p460

SUNDAY 10

My **power** word today is:

Choose a word from the power words on p460

Be the best friend you ever have.

OCTOBER

MONDAY 11

This week's focus:

My **power** word today is:

Choose a word from the power words on p460

My three most important tasks:

My other tasks:

My wish list:

Notes/reminders:

6am

7am

8am

9am

10am

11am

12 noon

1pm

2pm

3pm

4pm

5pm

6pm

7pm

8pm

9pm

10pm

Today I am grateful for:

Today I accomplished:

If you lose your temper you have lost the argument.

OCTOBER

TUESDAY 12

My **power** word today is:

Choose a word from the power words on p460

My three most important tasks:

My other tasks:

My wish list:

Notes/reminders:

6am

7am

8am

9am

10am

11am

12 noon

1pm

2pm

3pm

4pm

5pm

6pm

7pm

8pm

9pm

10pm

Today I am grateful for:

Today I accomplished:

The best antidote for worry is work.

OCTOBER

WEDNESDAY 13

My **power** word today is:

Choose a word from the power words on p460

My three most important tasks:

My other tasks:

My wish list:

Notes/reminders:

6am

7am

8am

9am

10am

11am

12 noon

1pm

2pm

3pm

4pm

5pm

6pm

7pm

8pm

9pm

10pm

Today I am grateful for:

Today I accomplished:

Be willing to get uncomfortable.

OCTOBER

THURSDAY 14

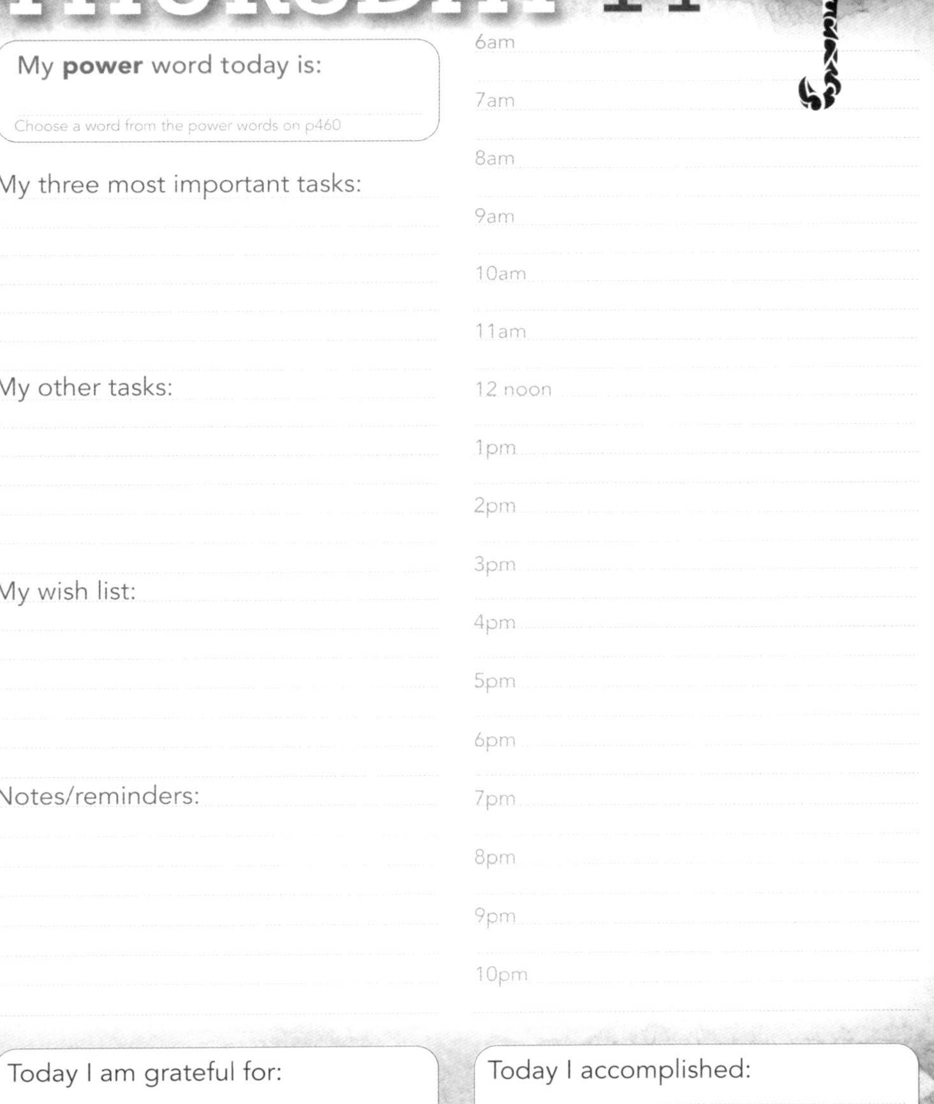

My **power** word today is:

Choose a word from the power words on p460

My three most important tasks:

My other tasks:

My wish list:

Notes/reminders:

6am

7am

8am

9am

10am

11am

12 noon

1pm

2pm

3pm

4pm

5pm

6pm

7pm

8pm

9pm

10pm

Today I am grateful for:

Today I accomplished:

Stretch yourself – you will increase your reach.

OCTOBER

FRIDAY 15

My **power** word today is:

Choose a word from the power words on p460

My three most important tasks:

My other tasks:

My wish list:

Notes/reminders:

6am

7am

8am

9am

10am

11am

12 noon

1pm

2pm

3pm

4pm

5pm

6pm

7pm

8pm

9pm

10pm

Today I am grateful for:

Today I accomplished:

Be willing to do what it takes.

SATURDAY 16

My **power** word today is:

Choose a word from the power words on p460

SUNDAY 17

My **power** word today is:

Choose a word from the power words on p460

Always give a little more than is expected of you.

OCTOBER

MONDAY 18

This week's focus:

My **power** word today is:

Choose a word from the power words on p460

My three most important tasks:

My other tasks:

My wish list:

Notes/reminders:

6am

7am

8am

9am

10am

11am

12 noon

1pm

2pm

3pm

4pm

5pm

6pm

7pm

8pm

9pm

10pm

Today I am grateful for:

Today I accomplished:

The mind heals with laughter.

OCTOBER

TUESDAY 19

My **power** word today is:

Choose a word from the power words on p460

My three most important tasks:

My other tasks:

My wish list:

Notes/reminders:

6am

7am

8am

9am

10am

11am

12 noon

1pm

2pm

3pm

4pm

5pm

6pm

7pm

8pm

9pm

10pm

Today I am grateful for:

Today I accomplished:

There are many precious moments beyond current circumstances.

OCTOBER

WEDNESDAY 20

My **power** word today is:

Choose a word from the power words on p460

My three most important tasks:

My other tasks:

My wish list:

Notes/reminders:

6am

7am

8am

9am

10am

11am

12 noon

1pm

2pm

3pm

4pm

5pm

6pm

7pm

8pm

9pm

10pm

Today I am grateful for:

Today I accomplished:

You can always change your mind.

OCTOBER

THURSDAY 21

My **power** word today is:

Choose a word from the power words on p460

My three most important tasks:

My other tasks:

My wish list:

Notes/reminders:

6am

7am

8am

9am

10am

11am

12 noon

1pm

2pm

3pm

4pm

5pm

6pm

7pm

8pm

9pm

10pm

Today I am grateful for:

Today I accomplished:

Everyone has something of value to contribute.

OCTOBER

FRIDAY 22

My **power** word today is:

Choose a word from the power words on p460

My three most important tasks:

My other tasks:

My wish list:

Notes/reminders:

6am

7am

8am

9am

10am

11am

12 noon

1pm

2pm

3pm

4pm

5pm

6pm

7pm

8pm

9pm

10pm

Today I am grateful for:

Today I accomplished:

Listen for the gold.

OCTOBER

SATURDAY 23

My **power** word today is:

Choose a word from the power words on p460

SUNDAY 24

My **power** word today is:

Choose a word from the power words on p460

Create a vision board of how you want your life to look.

OCTOBER • Bank Holiday

MONDAY 25

This week's focus:

My **power** word today is:

Choose a word from the power words on p460

My three most important tasks:

My other tasks:

My wish list:

Notes/reminders:

6am

7am

8am

9am

10am

11am

12 noon

1pm

2pm

3pm

4pm

5pm

6pm

7pm

8pm

9pm

10pm

Today I am grateful for:

Today I accomplished:

Acknowledge all of your accomplishments to date.

OCTOBER

TUESDAY 26

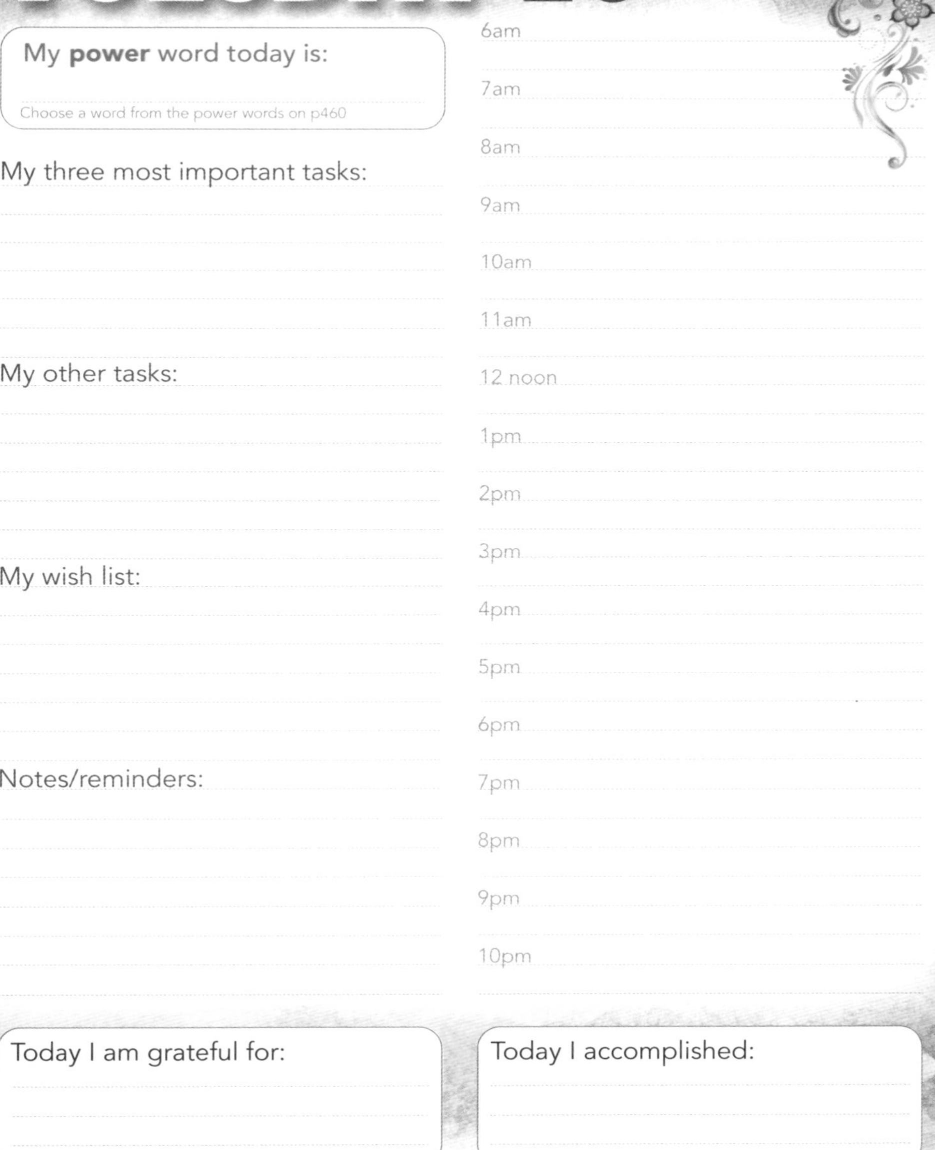

My **power** word today is:

Choose a word from the power words on p460

My three most important tasks:

My other tasks:

My wish list:

Notes/reminders:

6am

7am

8am

9am

10am

11am

12 noon

1pm

2pm

3pm

4pm

5pm

6pm

7pm

8pm

9pm

10pm

Today I am grateful for:

Today I accomplished:

Let your desires, not your fears, be your guide.

OCTOBER

WEDNESDAY 27

My **power** word today is:

Choose a word from the power words on p460

My three most important tasks:

My other tasks:

My wish list:

Notes/reminders:

6am

7am

8am

9am

10am

11am

12 noon

1pm

2pm

3pm

4pm

5pm

6pm

7pm

8pm

9pm

10pm

Today I am grateful for:

Today I accomplished:

Be with people who bring out the best in you.

OCTOBER

THURSDAY 28

My **power** word today is:

Choose a word from the power words on p460

My three most important tasks:

My other tasks:

My wish list:

Notes/reminders:

6am

7am

8am

9am

10am

11am

12 noon

1pm

2pm

3pm

4pm

5pm

6pm

7pm

8pm

9pm

10pm

Today I am grateful for:

Today I accomplished:

We all see the world from our own point of view.

OCTOBER

FRIDAY 29

My **power** word today is:

Choose a word from the power words on p460

My three most important tasks:

My other tasks:

My wish list:

Notes/reminders:

6am

7am

8am

9am

10am

11am

12 noon

1pm

2pm

3pm

4pm

5pm

6pm

7pm

8pm

9pm

10pm

Today I am grateful for:

Today I accomplished:

Discipline is the bridge between goals and accomplishments.

SATURDAY 30

My **power** word today is:

Choose a word from the power words on p460

SUNDAY 31

My **power** word today is:

Choose a word from the power words on p460

Remember why you started.

OCTOBER

Monthly reflections

Dreams are renewable. No matter what our age or condition, there are still untapped possibilities within us and new beauty waiting to be born.

Dr Dale E Turner

Best moments:

Greatest accomplishments:

Toughest challenge:

Biggest learnings:

Progress towards ongoing goals:

Remember your 2021 promises and your BIG WHY.
Remind yourself of your motives on page 10.

NOVEMBER

You are in the perfect position to get there from here.

Abraham-Hicks

NOVEMBER

MONDAY	TUESDAY	WEDNESDAY	THURSDAY	FRIDAY	SATURDAY	SUNDAY
1	2	3	4	5	6	7
8	9	10	11	12	13	14
15	16	17	18	19	20	21
22	23	24	25	26	27	28
29	30					

NOVEMBER ACTION PLANNER

A goal is a dream with a deadline

Dates/days to celebrate:

Events to attend:

People to meet/follow up:

Appointments to keep:

Trips to plan:

Purchases/payments to make:

Friends/family to contact:

Movies to see/books to read:

NOVEMBER

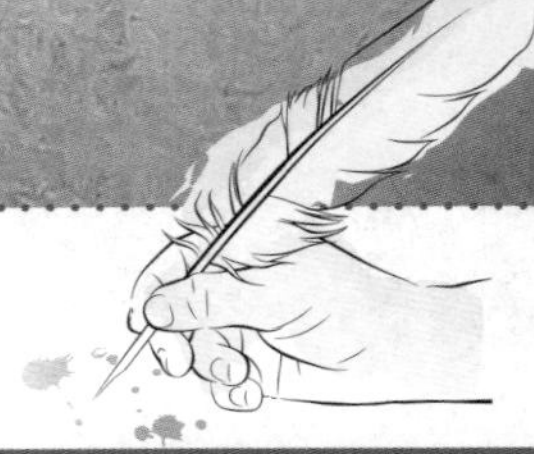

Monthly motivator

PRIORITIES

GOALS

CHALLENGES

ACTIONS

NOVEMBER

Financial tracker

MONTHLY CASH FLOW

	Personal	Business	Total
Income			
Salary			
Business dividend			
Pension			
Subsidy			
Other			
Total			
Living expenses			
Mortgage/rent			
Utilities/bills			
Credit card payments			
Loan repayments			
Insurance (home/car/life/health)			
Tax (personal/car/property)			
Savings			
Pension/investments			
House/garden			
Travel/fuel			
Groceries/toiletries			
Entertainment/dining out			
Education/training			
Child care			
Home care			
Health/self care/gym			
Other			
Total			
Total income			
Total outgoings			
Surplus/deficit			
This month's priority			

NOVEMBER

Food planner

A healthy outside starts from the inside.

MY MENU PLANNER (grocery list)

Week 1

Week 2

Week 3

Week 4

Reflections and comments:

This month's meal ideas:

A person who does not make time for wellness will surely need to take time for illness.

MY HEALTHY NUTRITION PLAN

	BREAKFAST	LUNCH	DINNER	SNACKS	FRUIT	VEGETABLES	WATER
Week 1							
Week 2							
Week 3							
Week 4							

Reflections and comments:

This month's healthy eating ideas:

NOVEMBER

Health planner

A man's health can be judged by what he takes two at a time – pills or stairs.

MY EXERCISE PLAN

	ACTIVITY	DURATION	HR	WT/BMI	NOTES
Week 1					
Week 2					
Week 3					
Week 4					

Reflections and comments:

This month's fitness goal:

Don't be afraid your life will end; be afraid that it will never begin.
Grace Hansen

MY WELLBEING PLAN

	PHYSICAL	MENTAL/EMOTIONAL	SOCIAL	FINANCIAL
Week 1				
Week 2				
Week 3				
Week 4				

Reflections and comments:

This month's wellbeing goal:

You start dying slowly
if you do not travel,
if you do not read,
if you do not listen to the sounds of life,
if you do not appreciate yourself.

You start dying slowly when you kill your
self-esteem, when you do not let others help you.

You start dying slowly if you become a slave to your
habits, walking everyday on the same paths,
if you do not change your routine,
if you do not wear different colours or you do not
speak to those you don't know.

You start dying slowly if you avoid passion and
its turbulent emotions, those that make your eyes
glisten and your heart beat fast.

You start dying slowly if you do not change your
life when you are not satisfied with your job, or
with your love, or with your surroundings.
If you do not risk what is safe for the uncertain,
if you do not go after a dream,
if you do not allow yourself,
at least once in your lifetime,
to run away from sensible advice.

Pablo Neruda

NOVEMBER

MONDAY 1

This week's focus:

My power word today is:

Choose a word from the power words on p460

My three most important tasks:

My other tasks:

My wish list:

Notes/reminders:

6am

7am

8am

9am

10am

11am

12 noon

1pm

2pm

3pm

4pm

5pm

6pm

7pm

8pm

9pm

10pm

Today I am grateful for:

Today I accomplished:

Your life is a hero's journey.

NOVEMBER

TUESDAY 2

My **power** word today is:

Choose a word from the power words on p460

My three most important tasks:

My other tasks:

My wish list:

Notes/reminders:

6am

7am

8am

9am

10am

11am

12 noon

1pm

2pm

3pm

4pm

5pm

6pm

7pm

8pm

9pm

10pm

Today I am grateful for:

Today I accomplished:

Put your best foot forward.

NOVEMBER

WEDNESDAY 3

My **power** word today is:

Choose a word from the power words on p460

My three most important tasks:

My other tasks:

My wish list:

Notes/reminders:

6am

7am

8am

9am

10am

11am

12 noon

1pm

2pm

3pm

4pm

5pm

6pm

7pm

8pm

9pm

10pm

Today I am grateful for:

Today I accomplished:

Let go of expectations.

NOVEMBER

THURSDAY 4

My **power** word today is:

Choose a word from the power words on p460

My three most important tasks:

My other tasks:

My wish list:

Notes/reminders:

6am

7am

8am

9am

10am

11am

12 noon

1pm

2pm

3pm

4pm

5pm

6pm

7pm

8pm

9pm

10pm

Today I am grateful for:

Today I accomplished:

Focus on excellence.

NOVEMBER

FRIDAY 5

My **power** word today is:

Choose a word from the power words on p460

6am

7am

8am

My three most important tasks:

9am

10am

11am

My other tasks:

12 noon

1pm

2pm

3pm

My wish list:

4pm

5pm

6pm

Notes/reminders:

7pm

8pm

9pm

10pm

Today I am grateful for:

Today I accomplished:

Put your passion into action.

SATURDAY 6

My **power** word today is:

Choose a word from the power words on p460

SUNDAY 7

My **power** word today is:

Choose a word from the power words on p460

Acknowledge your achievements.

NOVEMBER

MONDAY 8

This week's focus:

My **power** word today is:

Choose a word from the power words on p460

My three most important tasks:

My other tasks:

My wish list:

Notes/reminders:

6am

7am

8am

9am

10am

11am

12 noon

1pm

2pm

3pm

4pm

5pm

6pm

7pm

8pm

9pm

10pm

Today I am grateful for:

Today I accomplished:

Generosity starts with ourselves.

NOVEMBER

TUESDAY 9

My **power** word today is:

Choose a word from the power words on p460

Choose a word from the power words on p460

My three most important tasks:

My other tasks:

My wish list:

Notes/reminders:

6am

7am

8am

9am

10am

11am

12 noon

1pm

2pm

3pm

4pm

5pm

6pm

7pm

8pm

9pm

10pm

Today I am grateful for:

Today I accomplished:

Explore the limits of your comfort zone.

NOVEMBER

WEDNESDAY 10

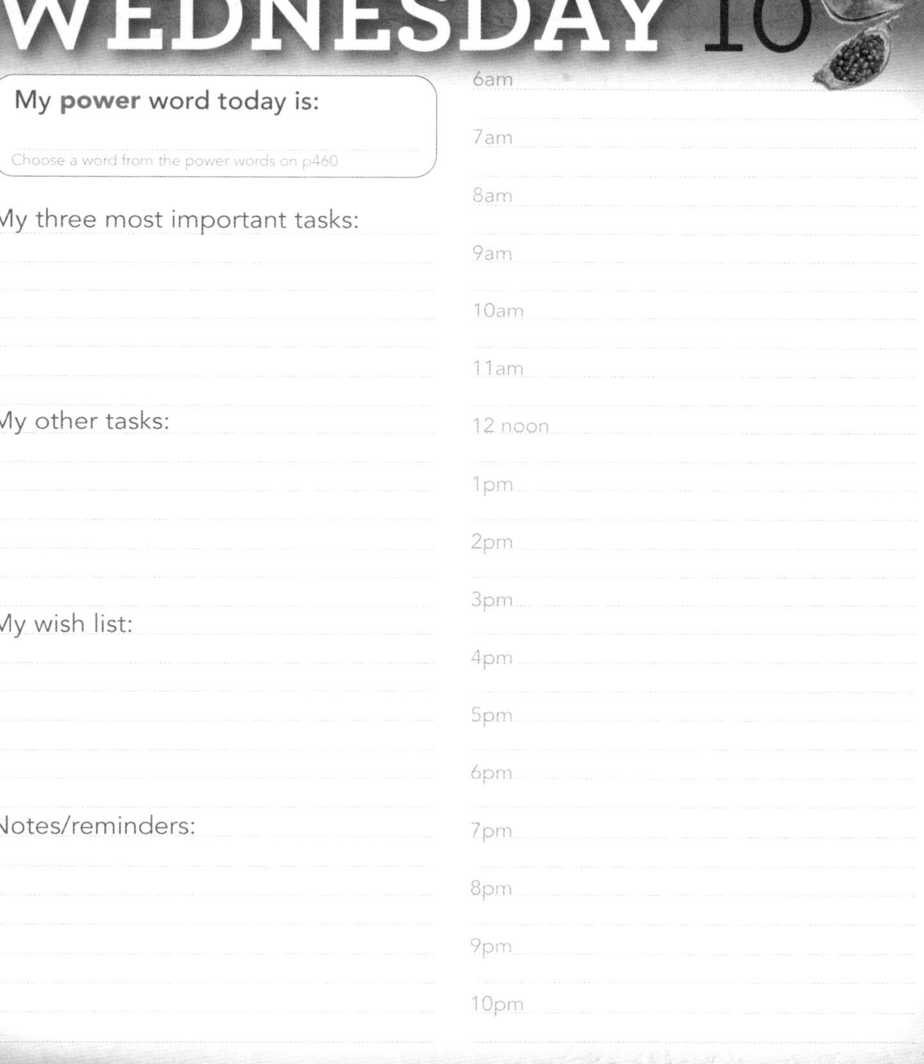

My **power** word today is:

Choose a word from the power words on p460

My three most important tasks:

My other tasks:

My wish list:

Notes/reminders:

6am

7am

8am

9am

10am

11am

12 noon

1pm

2pm

3pm

4pm

5pm

6pm

7pm

8pm

9pm

10pm

Today I am grateful for:

Today I accomplished:

Feel the fear and do it anyway.

NOVEMBER

THURSDAY 11

My power word today is:

Choose a word from the power words on p460

My three most important tasks:

My other tasks:

My wish list:

Notes/reminders:

6am

7am

8am

9am

10am

11am

12 noon

1pm

2pm

3pm

4pm

5pm

6pm

7pm

8pm

9pm

10pm

Today I am grateful for:

Today I accomplished:

Stretch the limits of your thinking.

NOVEMBER

FRIDAY 12

My **power** word today is:

Choose a word from the power words on p460

My three most important tasks:

My other tasks:

My wish list:

Notes/reminders:

6am

7am

8am

9am

10am

11am

12 noon

1pm

2pm

3pm

4pm

5pm

6pm

7pm

8pm

9pm

10pm

Today I am grateful for:

Today I accomplished:

If you're not expanding, you're contracting.

NOVEMBER

SATURDAY 13

My **power** word today is:

Choose a word from the power words on p460

SUNDAY 14

My **power** word today is:

Choose a word from the power words on p460

Practice healthy thinking.

NOVEMBER

MONDAY 15

This week's focus:

My **power** word today is:

Choose a word from the power words on p460

My three most important tasks:

My other tasks:

My wish list:

Notes/reminders:

6am

7am

8am

9am

10am

11am

12 noon

1pm

2pm

3pm

4pm

5pm

6pm

7pm

8pm

9pm

10pm

Today I am grateful for:

Today I accomplished:

Have a bigger why.

NOVEMBER

TUESDAY 16

My **power** word today is:

Choose a word from the power words on p460

My three most important tasks:

My other tasks:

My wish list:

Notes/reminders:

6am

7am

8am

9am

10am

11am

12 noon

1pm

2pm

3pm

4pm

5pm

6pm

7pm

8pm

9pm

10pm

Today I am grateful for:

Today I accomplished:

Be proud of your game.

NOVEMBER

WEDNESDAY 17

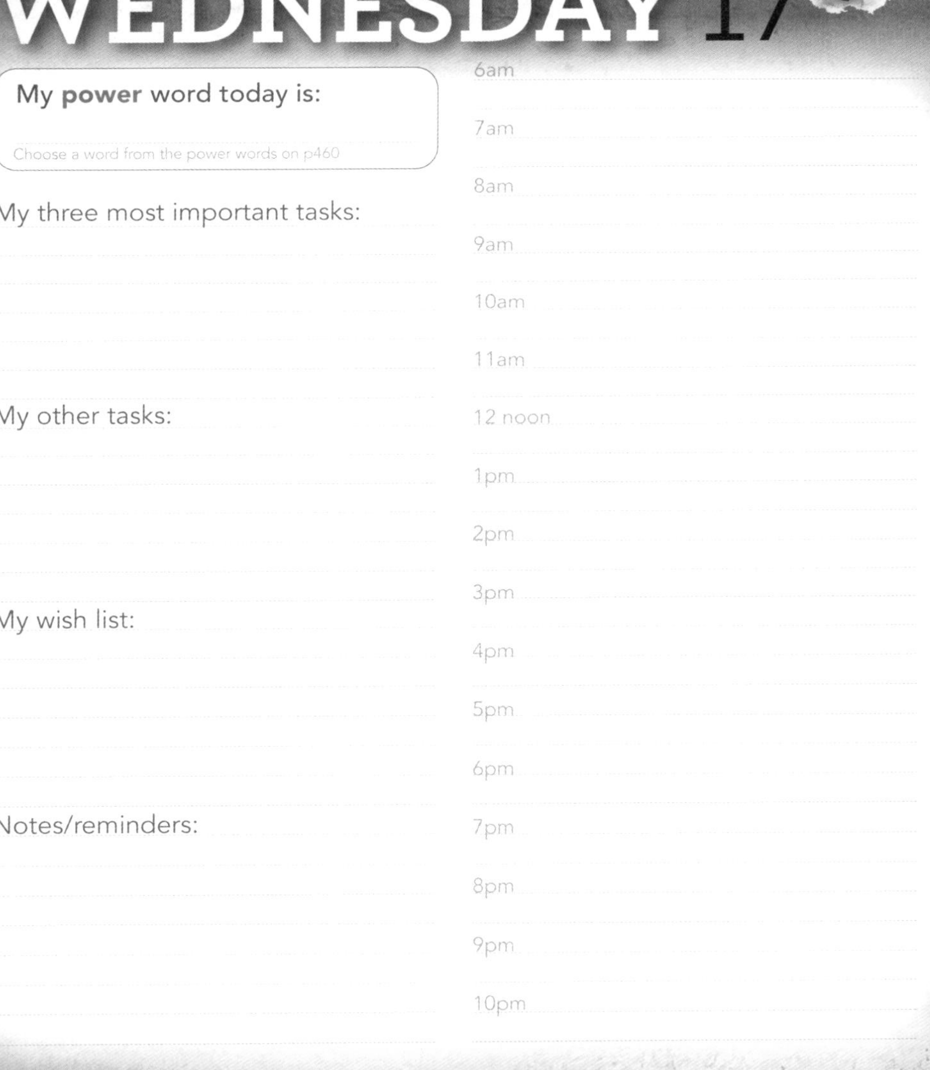

My **power** word today is:

Choose a word from the power words on p460

My three most important tasks:

My other tasks:

My wish list:

Notes/reminders:

6am

7am

8am

9am

10am

11am

12 noon

1pm

2pm

3pm

4pm

5pm

6pm

7pm

8pm

9pm

10pm

Today I am grateful for:

Today I accomplished:

Chose your friends wisely.

NOVEMBER

THURSDAY 18

My **power** word today is:

Choose a word from the power words on p460

My three most important tasks:

My other tasks:

My wish list:

Notes/reminders:

6am

7am

8am

9am

10am

11am

12 noon

1pm

2pm

3pm

4pm

5pm

6pm

7pm

8pm

9pm

10pm

Today I am grateful for:

Today I accomplished:

You are responsible for your own journey.

NOVEMBER

FRIDAY 19

My **power** word today is:

Choose a word from the power words on p460

My three most important tasks:

My other tasks:

My wish list:

Notes/reminders:

6am

7am

8am

9am

10am

11am

12 noon

1pm

2pm

3pm

4pm

5pm

6pm

7pm

8pm

9pm

10pm

Today I am grateful for:

Today I accomplished:

Sort out your priorities.

NOVEMBER

SATURDAY 20

My **power** word today is:

Choose a word from the power words on p460

SUNDAY 21

My **power** word today is:

Choose a word from the power words on p460

Get rid of excuses.

NOVEMBER

MONDAY 22

This week's focus:

My **power** word today is:

Choose a word from the power words on p460

My three most important tasks:

My other tasks:

My wish list:

Notes/reminders:

6am

7am

8am

9am

10am

11am

12 noon

1pm

2pm

3pm

4pm

5pm

6pm

7pm

8pm

9pm

10pm

Today I am grateful for:

Today I accomplished:

Master your emotions or they will master you.

NOVEMBER

TUESDAY 23

My power word today is:

Choose a word from the power words on p460

My three most important tasks:

My other tasks:

My wish list:

Notes/reminders:

6am

7am

8am

9am

10am

11am

12 noon

1pm

2pm

3pm

4pm

5pm

6pm

7pm

8pm

9pm

10pm

Today I am grateful for:

Today I accomplished:

Let failure point you to success.

NOVEMBER

WEDNESDAY 24

My power word today is:

Choose a word from the power words on p460

My three most important tasks:

My other tasks:

My wish list:

Notes/reminders:

6am

7am

8am

9am

10am

11am

12 noon

1pm

2pm

3pm

4pm

5pm

6pm

7pm

8pm

9pm

10pm

Today I am grateful for:

Today I accomplished:

90% of those who fail are not defeated – they quit.

NOVEMBER

THURSDAY 25

My **power** word today is:

Choose a word from the power words on p460

My three most important tasks:

My other tasks:

My wish list:

Notes/reminders:

6am

7am

8am

9am

10am

11am

12 noon

1pm

2pm

3pm

4pm

5pm

6pm

7pm

8pm

9pm

10pm

Today I am grateful for:

Today I accomplished:

Look for the solution in every challenge.

NOVEMBER

FRIDAY 26

My **power** word today is:

Choose a word from the power words on p460

My three most important tasks:

My other tasks:

My wish list:

Notes/reminders:

6am

7am

8am

9am

10am

11am

12 noon

1pm

2pm

3pm

4pm

5pm

6pm

7pm

8pm

9pm

10pm

Today I am grateful for:

Today I accomplished:

Criticism gets you nowhere.

NOVEMBER

SATURDAY 27

My **power** word today is:

Choose a word from the power words on p460

SUNDAY 28

My **power** word today is:

Choose a word from the power words on p460

Recognise your strengths.

NOVEMBER

MONDAY 29

This week's focus:

My **power** word today is:

Choose a word from the power words on p460

My three most important tasks:

My other tasks:

My wish list:

Notes/reminders:

6am

7am

8am

9am

10am

11am

12 noon

1pm

2pm

3pm

4pm

5pm

6pm

7pm

8pm

9pm

10pm

Today I am grateful for:

Today I accomplished:

Believe in your ability to learn.

NOVEMBER

TUESDAY 30

My power word today is:

Choose a word from the power words on p460

My three most important tasks:

My other tasks:

My wish list:

Notes/reminders:

6am

7am

8am

9am

10am

11am

12 noon

1pm

2pm

3pm

4pm

5pm

6pm

7pm

8pm

9pm

10pm

Today I am grateful for:

Today I accomplished:

Tap into your natural passion.

PEACE MAKING

THE ESSENTIALS OF CONFLICT RESOLUTION

- Slow down the action. Take a deep breath. Count to 10.
- Be willing to give the other person the benefit of the doubt.
- Trust that a win-win solution is possible and best for everyone.
- Listen fully to understand the other's point of view.
- Listening is not the same as agreeing. There is no need to interrupt or contradict. You will have your turn.
- Acknowledge the other persons feelings – this reassures them you're listening.
- Be straight without being defensive or attacking – this helps the other to listen.
- See a conflict as a problem to be solved not a battle to be won.
- Set your sights on a win-win solution so both leave listened to, heard and happy.
- Ask for neutral perspective if you're getting stuck or triggered.
- Remember that conflict is an opportunity for growth
- Listening to others' views is a great way to hear new ideas and deepen your understanding of a situation, circumstance or person.
- The heroes and heroines our world needs most are those with the courage and intelligence to handle conflict creatively and peacefully.

NOVEMBER

Doodles and ideas

5 TIPS FOR PEACE OF MIND

- Let go of anger
- Let go of regret
- Let go of resentment
- Let go of guilt or shame
- Forgive and forget

NOVEMBER

Monthly reflections

Reach high, for stars lie hidden in your soul. Dream deep, for every dream precedes the goal.
Pamela Vaull Starr

Best moments:

Greatest accomplishments:

Toughest challenge:

Biggest learnings:

Progress towards ongoing goals:

Remember your 2021 promises and your BIG WHY.
Remind yourself of your motives on page 10.

DECEMBER

Christmas wish list

5 TIPS FOR A GREAT LIFE

- Be courageous
- Be authentic
- Be responsible
- Be grateful
- Be happy

DECEMBER

All things are difficult before they are easy.

Thomas Fuller

DECEMBER

AT A GLANCE

MONDAY	TUESDAY	WEDNESDAY	THURSDAY	FRIDAY	SATURDAY	SUNDAY
		1	2	3	4	5
6	7	8	9	10	11	12
13	14	15	16	17	18	19
20	21	22	23	24	25	26
27	28	29	30	31		

DECEMBER ACTION PLANNER

A goal is a dream with a deadline

Dates/days to celebrate:

Events to attend:

People to meet/follow up:

Appointments to keep:

Trips to plan:

Purchases/payments to make:

Friends/family to contact:

Movies to see/books to read:

DECEMBER

Monthly motivator

PRIORITIES

GOALS

CHALLENGES

ACTIONS

DECEMBER

Financial tracker

MONTHLY CASH FLOW

	Personal	Business	Total
Income			
Salary			
Business dividend			
Pension			
Subsidy			
Other			
Total			
Living expenses			
Mortgage/rent			
Utilities/bills			
Credit card payments			
Loan repayments			
Insurance (home/car/life/health)			
Tax (personal/car/property)			
Savings			
Pension/investments			
House/garden			
Travel/fuel			
Groceries/toiletries			
Entertainment/dining out			
Education/training			
Child care			
Home care			
Health/self care/gym			
Other			
Total			
Total income			
Total outgoings			
Surplus/deficit			
This month's priority			

DECEMBER

Food planner

Food is fuel – with therapeutic potential.

MY MENU PLANNER (grocery list)

Week 1

Week 2

Week 3

Week 4

Reflections and comments:

This month's meal ideas:

About 80% of the food on shelves of supermarkets today didn't exist 100 years ago.

MY HEALTHY NUTRITION PLAN

	BREAKFAST	LUNCH	DINNER	SNACKS	FRUIT	VEGETABLES	WATER
Week 1							
Week 2							
Week 3							
Week 4							

Reflections and comments:

This month's healthy eating ideas:

DECEMBER

Health planner

Better to do something imperfectly than to do nothing flawlessly.

MY EXERCISE PLAN

	ACTIVITY	DURATION	HR	WT/BMI	NOTES
Week 1					
Week 2					
Week 3					
Week 4					

Reflections and comments:

This month's fitness goal:

All you need is love. But a little chocolate now and then doesn't hurt.

MY WELLBEING PLAN

	PHYSICAL	MENTAL/EMOTIONAL	SOCIAL	FINANCIAL
Week 1				
Week 2				
Week 3				
Week 4				

Reflections and comments:

This month's wellbeing goal:

GRATITUDE GUIDE

I'm grateful for:

A personal strength:

A relationship I value:

A family trait:

A skill I learned:

Something I have that money can't buy:

A gift I received:

A source of comfort:

Something in nature:

A lesson I learned:

A change I made:

A unique feature about me:

A memory I cherish:

A challenge I overcame:

An experience I had:

A person I met:

A risk I took:

An interesting discovery I made:

An opportunity I had:

A result I achieved:

Something beautiful in my life:

A contribution I made:

A real stroke of luck:

DECEMBER

WEDNESDAY 1

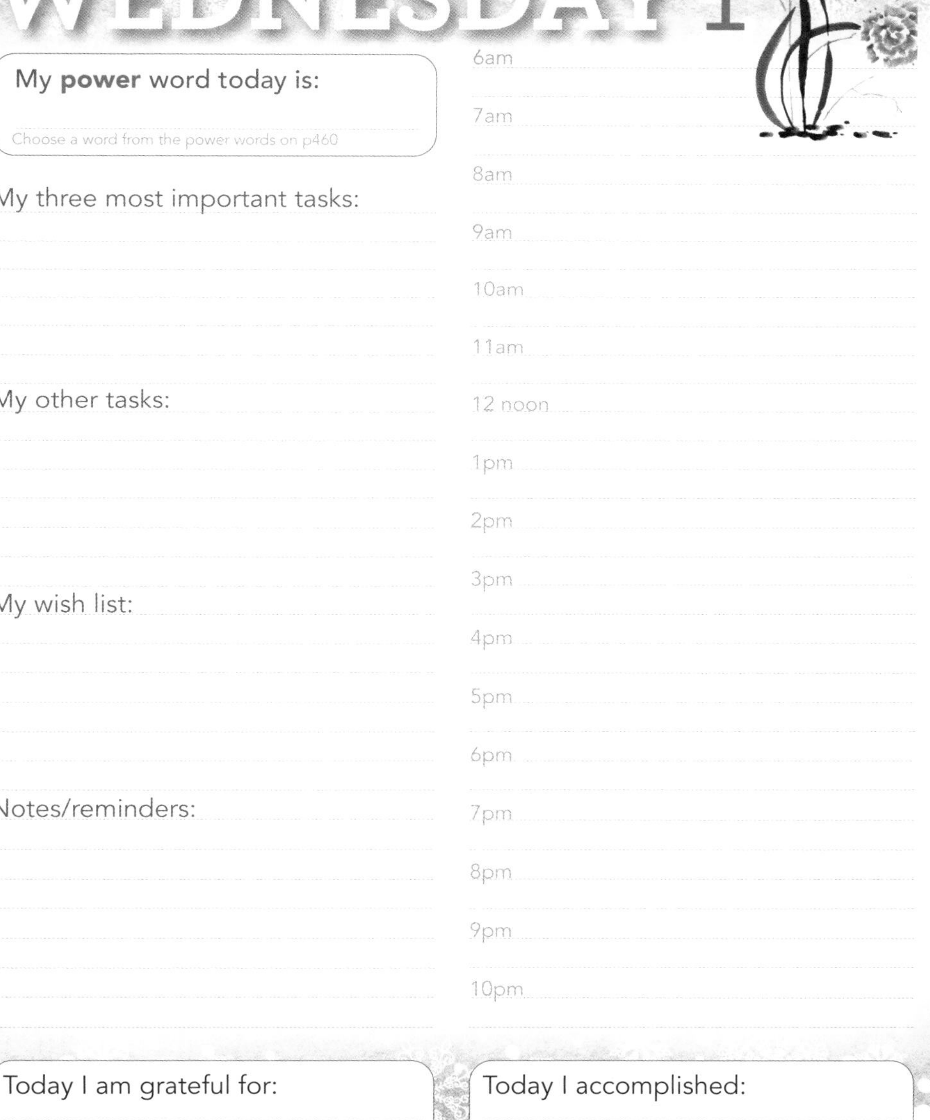

My **power** word today is:

Choose a word from the power words on p460

My three most important tasks:

My other tasks:

My wish list:

Notes/reminders:

6am

7am

8am

9am

10am

11am

12 noon

1pm

2pm

3pm

4pm

5pm

6pm

7pm

8pm

9pm

10pm

Today I am grateful for:

Today I accomplished:

Two heads are better than one.

DECEMBER

THURSDAY 2

My **power** word today is:

Choose a word from the power words on p460

My three most important tasks:

My other tasks:

My wish list:

Notes/reminders:

6am

7am

8am

9am

10am

11am

12 noon

1pm

2pm

3pm

4pm

5pm

6pm

7pm

8pm

9pm

10pm

Today I am grateful for:

Today I accomplished:

Empower your dreams in the pursuit of them.

DECEMBER

FRIDAY 3

My **power** word today is:

Choose a word from the power words on p460

My three most important tasks:

My other tasks:

My wish list:

Notes/reminders:

6am

7am

8am

9am

10am

11am

12 noon

1pm

2pm

3pm

4pm

5pm

6pm

7pm

8pm

9pm

10pm

Today I am grateful for:

Today I accomplished:

Spend time with enthusiastic people.

SATURDAY 4

My **power** word today is:

Choose a word from the power words on p460

SUNDAY 5

My **power** word today is:

Choose a word from the power words on p460

Your vision is in your mind's eye.

DECEMBER

MONDAY 6

This week's focus:

My **power** word today is:

Choose a word from the power words on p460

6am

7am

8am

9am

10am

11am

12 noon

1pm

2pm

3pm

4pm

5pm

6pm

7pm

8pm

9pm

10pm

My three most important tasks:

My other tasks:

My wish list:

Notes/reminders:

Today I am grateful for:

Today I accomplished:

Develop the talent you have.

TUESDAY 7

My **power** word today is:

Choose a word from the power words on p460

My three most important tasks:

My other tasks:

My wish list:

Notes/reminders:

6am

7am

8am

9am

10am

11am

12 noon

1pm

2pm

3pm

4pm

5pm

6pm

7pm

8pm

9pm

10pm

Today I am grateful for:

Today I accomplished:

Bring more fun to the workplace.

WEDNESDAY 8

My **power** word today is:

Choose a word from the power words on p460

My three most important tasks:

My other tasks:

My wish list:

Notes/reminders:

6am

7am

8am

9am

10am

11am

12 noon

1pm

2pm

3pm

4pm

5pm

6pm

7pm

8pm

9pm

10pm

Today I am grateful for:

Today I accomplished:

Anything is possible in a conversation.

THURSDAY 9

My **power** word today is:

Choose a word from the power words on p460

My three most important tasks:

My other tasks:

My wish list:

Notes/reminders:

6am

7am

8am

9am

10am

11am

12 noon

1pm

2pm

3pm

4pm

5pm

6pm

7pm

8pm

9pm

10pm

Today I am grateful for:

Today I accomplished:

Encourage the dreams of others.

DECEMBER

FRIDAY 10

My **power** word today is:

Choose a word from the power words on p460

My three most important tasks:

My other tasks:

My wish list:

Notes/reminders:

6am

7am

8am

9am

10am

11am

12 noon

1pm

2pm

3pm

4pm

5pm

6pm

7pm

8pm

9pm

10pm

Today I am grateful for:

Today I accomplished:

Do what you know to do.

SATURDAY 11

My **power** word today is:

Choose a word from the power words on p460

SUNDAY 12

My **power** word today is:

Choose a word from the power words on p460

Be prepared for surprises.

DECEMBER

MONDAY 13

This week's focus:

My **power** word today is:

Choose a word from the power words on p460

My three most important tasks:

My other tasks:

My wish list:

Notes/reminders:

6am

7am

8am

9am

10am

11am

12 noon

1pm

2pm

3pm

4pm

5pm

6pm

7pm

8pm

9pm

10pm

Today I am grateful for:

Today I accomplished:

Stay open and curious.

DECEMBER

TUESDAY 14

My **power** word today is:

Choose a word from the power words on p460

My three most important tasks:

My other tasks:

My wish list:

Notes/reminders:

6am

7am

8am

9am

10am

11am

12 noon

1pm

2pm

3pm

4pm

5pm

6pm

7pm

8pm

9pm

10pm

Today I am grateful for:

Today I accomplished:

Do not be afraid to fail.

DECEMBER

WEDNESDAY 15

My **power** word today is:

Choose a word from the power words on p460

My three most important tasks:

My other tasks:

My wish list:

Notes/reminders:

6am

7am

8am

9am

10am

11am

12 noon

1pm

2pm

3pm

4pm

5pm

6pm

7pm

8pm

9pm

10pm

Today I am grateful for:

Today I accomplished:

Success does not require misery.

DECEMBER

THURSDAY 16

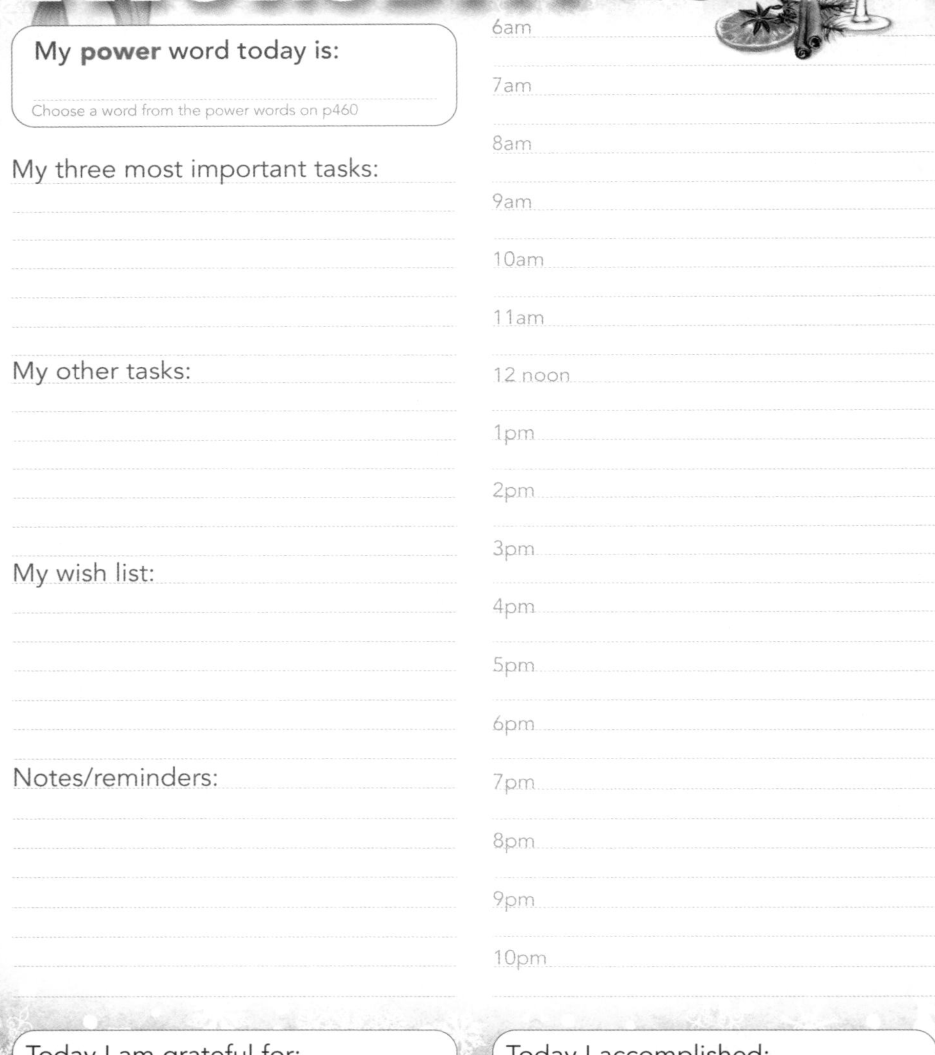

My **power** word today is:

Choose a word from the power words on p460

My three most important tasks:

My other tasks:

My wish list:

Notes/reminders:

6am

7am

8am

9am

10am

11am

12 noon

1pm

2pm

3pm

4pm

5pm

6pm

7pm

8pm

9pm

10pm

Today I am grateful for:

Today I accomplished:

Create a life worth loving.

DECEMBER

FRIDAY 17

My **power** word today is:

Choose a word from the power words on p460

My three most important tasks:

My other tasks:

My wish list:

Notes/reminders:

6am

7am

8am

9am

10am

11am

12 noon

1pm

2pm

3pm

4pm

5pm

6pm

7pm

8pm

9pm

10pm

Today I am grateful for:

Today I accomplished:

Your best contribution is a good mood.

SATURDAY 18

My **power** word today is:

Choose a word from the power words on p460

SUNDAY 19

My **power** word today is:

Choose a word from the power words on p460

Put your dreams to work for you.

DECEMBER

MONDAY 20

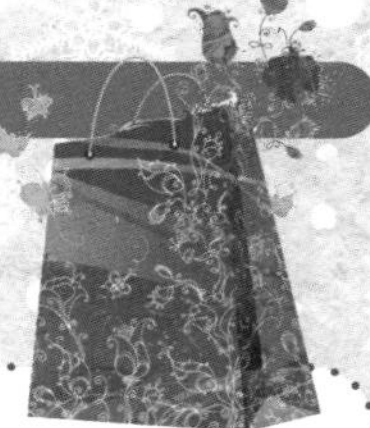

This week's focus:

My **power** word today is:

Choose a word from the power words on p460

My three most important tasks:

My other tasks:

My wish list:

Notes/reminders:

6am

7am

8am

9am

10am

11am

12 noon

1pm

2pm

3pm

4pm

5pm

6pm

7pm

8pm

9pm

10pm

Today I am grateful for:

Today I accomplished:

Sometimes it is wise to be discontent with the status quo.

DECEMBER

TUESDAY 21

My power word today is:

Choose a word from the power words on p460

My three most important tasks:

My other tasks:

My wish list:

Notes/reminders:

6am

7am

8am

9am

10am

11am

12 noon

1pm

2pm

3pm

4pm

5pm

6pm

7pm

8pm

9pm

10pm

Today I am grateful for:

Today I accomplished:

Add value wherever you are.

DECEMBER

WEDNESDAY 22

My **power** word today is:

Choose a word from the power words on p460

on p460

My three most important tasks:

My other tasks:

My wish list:

Notes/reminders:

6am

7am

8am

9am

10am

11am

12 noon

1pm

2pm

3pm

4pm

5pm

6pm

7pm

8pm

9pm

10pm

Today I am grateful for:

Today I accomplished:

Don't worry; be happy.

DECEMBER

THURSDAY 23

My **power** word today is:

Choose a word from the power words on p460

My three most important tasks:

My other tasks:

My wish list:

Notes/reminders:

6am

7am

8am

9am

10am

11am

12 noon

1pm

2pm

3pm

4pm

5pm

6pm

7pm

8pm

9pm

10pm

Today I am grateful for:

Today I accomplished:

We cannot succeed alone.

DECEMBER • Christmas Eve

FRIDAY 24

My **power** word today is:

Choose a word from the power words on p460

My three most important tasks:

My other tasks:

My wish list:

Notes/reminders:

6am

7am

8am

9am

10am

11am

12 noon

1pm

2pm

3pm

4pm

5pm

6pm

7pm

8pm

9pm

10pm

Today I am grateful for:

Today I accomplished:

Have a personal mission statement for your life.

DECEMBER • Christmas Day

SATURDAY 25

My **power** word today is:

Choose a word from the power words on p460

SUNDAY 26 St Stephen's Day

My **power** word today is:

Choose a word from the power words on p460

Courage and confidence grow from within.

DECEMBER

MONDAY 27

This week's focus:

My **power** word today is:

Choose a word from the power words on p460

My three most important tasks:

My other tasks:

My wish list:

Notes/reminders:

6am

7am

8am

9am

10am

11am

12 noon

1pm

2pm

3pm

4pm

5pm

6pm

7pm

8pm

9pm

10pm

Today I am grateful for:

Today I accomplished:

Get to know the person in the mirror.

DECEMBER

TUESDAY 28

My **power** word today is:

Choose a word from the power words on p460

My three most important tasks:

My other tasks:

My wish list:

Notes/reminders:

6am

7am

8am

9am

10am

11am

12 noon

1pm

2pm

3pm

4pm

5pm

6pm

7pm

8pm

9pm

10pm

Today I am grateful for:

Today I accomplished:

When principle is involved, don't budge.

DECEMBER

WEDNESDAY 29

My **power** word today is:

Choose a word from the power words on p460

My three most important tasks:

My other tasks:

My wish list:

Notes/reminders:

6am

7am

8am

9am

10am

11am

12 noon

1pm

2pm

3pm

4pm

5pm

6pm

7pm

8pm

9pm

10pm

Today I am grateful for:

Today I accomplished:

It pays to listen.

DECEMBER

THURSDAY 30

My **power** word today is:

Choose a word from the power words on p460

My three most important tasks:

My other tasks:

My wish list:

Notes/reminders:

6am

7am

8am

9am

10am

11am

12 noon

1pm

2pm

3pm

4pm

5pm

6pm

7pm

8pm

9pm

10pm

Today I am grateful for:

Today I accomplished:

Do what you love, the reward will follow.

DECEMBER • New Year's Eve

FRIDAY 31

My **power** word today is:

Choose a word from the power words on p460

My three most important tasks:

My other tasks:

My wish list:

Notes/reminders:

6am

7am

8am

9am

10am

11am

12 noon

1pm

2pm

3pm

4pm

5pm

6pm

7pm

8pm

9pm

10pm

Today I am grateful for:

Today I accomplished:

Encourage others.

DECEMBER

Wheel of life

MY SATISFACTION RATING

Indicate your % on the circle: Give yourself a score between 0% and 100% on each section Compare to January's *Wheel of life* on page 15 to see your progress and satisfaction rating

Leisure/ social life — 100%
Learning/ personal growth — 100%
Family/home environment — 100%
Self care/ stress mastery — 100%
Money/financial planning — 100%
Health/ vitality — 100%
Career/ work — 100%
Nutrition/ exercise — 100%
Life purpose/ fulfilment — 100%
Relationships/ intimacy — 100%
Contribution/ spirituality — 100%
Self image/ self esteem — 100%

0%

Areas to work on/improve:

DECEMBER

Monthly reflections

A year from now you may wish you had started today.
Karen Lamb

Best moments:

Greatest accomplishments:

Toughest challenge:

Biggest learnings:

Progress towards ongoing goals:

Remember your 2021 promises and your BIG WHY.
Remind yourself of your motives on page 10.
It's time to create your 2022 promises and a new BIG WHY.

Quarterly check-in

YES	NO	
☐	☐	Are you eating in a way that supports your good health?
☐	☐	Are you getting enough sleep?
☐	☐	Are you participating in regular physical exercise?
☐	☐	Are you managing your finances?
☐	☐	Are you enjoying your work/career?
☐	☐	Are you caring for yourself responsibly?
☐	☐	Are you engaged with your community?
☐	☐	Are you meeting friends and family frequently?
☐	☐	Are you journaling/painting/writing/dancing/ singing?
☐	☐	Is your house/car/office/desk tidy?
☐	☐	Is your communication clear and straight?
☐	☐	Are you satisfied with how you are living your life?
☐	☐	Are you avoiding anything/anyone?
☐	☐	Are you ignoring/resisting anything?
☐	☐	Are you being a good role model in your life?
☐	☐	Are your relationships/partnerships thriving?
☐	☐	Are you growing in courage and confidence?
☐	☐	Are you taking on new challenges with interest?
☐	☐	Are you curious and excited about the future?
☐	☐	Are you working towards fulfilling your dreams?

Areas to work on/improve in the next three months:

RESOLUTIONS FOR THE NEW YEAR

Drink more water.
Prioritise eco-friendly choices.
Volunteer to fundraise for a worthy cause.
Adopt an attitude of gratitude.
Spend 10 minutes a day tidying.
Set your alarm for the same time each day.
Develop a skin care routine.
Become a more aware consumer.
Perfect one recipe.
Set up a monthly budget.
Schedule time for silence.
Attend a new class.
Take more frequent breaks.
Practice mindful breathing.
Make plans to explore more.
Ditch one bad habit.
Create a bed time routine.
Make time for fun.
Embrace spontaneity.
Clean out your inbox.
Start a dream journal.
Plan a new adventure.
Create a balanced work/play/sleep (8-8-8) life.
Do regular random acts of kindness.
Live a life you love.

102 power words

Acceptance
Action
Awareness
Adventure
Accountability
Authenticity
Balance
Bravery
Brilliance
Beauty
Contribution
Confidence
Clarity
Calm
Courage
Choice
Connection
Creativity
Collaboration
Commitment
Compassion
Curiosity
Decisive
Daring
Discovery
Dedication
Dignity
Enthusiasm
Energy
Excitement
Encouragement
Fun
Freedom
Forgiveness

Focus
Fairness
Flexibility
Gratitude
Growth
Generosity
Goodness
Harmony
Honesty
Healing
Humility
Honour
Happiness
Intuition
Integrity
Inspiration
Intention
Joy
Justice
Kindness
Knowing
Listening
Loyalty
Love
Learning
Leadership
Miracles
Motivate
Mastery
Magnificence
Natural
Nurturing
Optimistic
Open

Opportunity
Partnership
Presence
Promise
Persistence
Participation
Peaceful
Possibility
Powerful
Playful
Question
Quiet
Resilience
Resourcefulness
Responsibility
Reflection
Respect
Strength
Support
Sharing
Service
Trust
Truth
Team
Talent
Useful
Universal
Unique
Vision
Vitality
Versatile
Wonder
Wisdom
Workability

Project/event planning check-list

Name of project:

Project leader:

Team leader:

Date of event:

Venue:

Location:

Capacity:

Purpose:

Objectives:

Desired outcome:

- [ ] Team
- [ ] Budget
- [ ] Resources
- [ ] Schedule of meetings
- [ ] Task list
- [ ] Timeline
- [ ] Milestones
- [ ] Communication plan
- [ ] Contact list
- [ ] Stakeholders
- [ ] Sponsors
- [ ] Partners
- [ ] Investors
- [ ] Progress report
- [ ] Communication plan
- [ ] VIPs
- [ ] Speakers
- [ ] Contracts
- [ ] Registration process
- [ ] PR/advertising
- [ ] Marketing
- [ ] Tickets/track sales
- [ ] Catering
- [ ] Audio visual
- [ ] Parking
- [ ] Signage
- [ ] Legal
- [ ] Health and safety
- [ ] Insurance
- [ ] Photography
- [ ] Follow-up
- [ ] Evaluation
- [ ] Acknowledgement
- [ ] Define team roles/responsibilites

Holiday check-list

Choose joy

Destinations:

Adventures:

Experiences:

Concerns:

PREPARATION FOR THE TRIP

- [ ] Passport
- [ ] Visa requirements
- [ ] Travel insurance/policy no
- [ ] Health insurance/policy no
- [ ] Savings plan
- [ ] Travel vaccinations
- [ ] Credit cards
- [ ] Local currency
- [ ] Bank details
- [ ] Key with neighbour
- [ ] International driver's permit
- [ ] Passenger tickets
- [ ] Accommodation reservation
- [ ] Copies of relevant documents
- [ ] International voltage adaptor
- [ ] Phone/IPAD/laptop
- [ ] Charger
- [ ] Camera
- [ ] Medicine
- [ ] Glasses/contact lenses
- [ ] Baby wipes/cleanser
- [ ] Cosmetics
- [ ] Sunscreen
- [ ] Sewing kit
- [ ] Scissors
- [ ] Torch

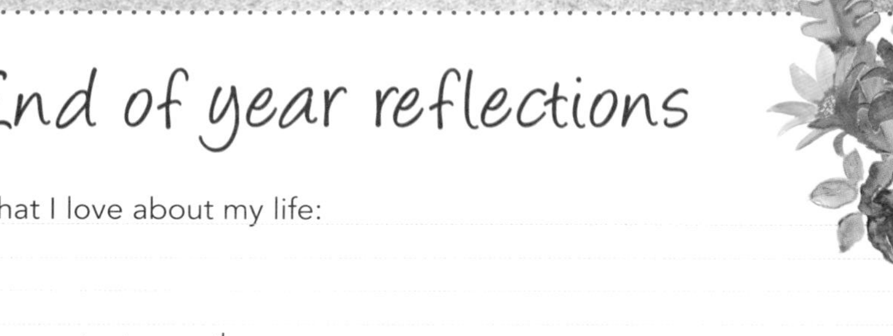

End of year reflections

What I love about my life:

My greatest growth:

My toughest challenges:

My proudest accomplishments:

My three biggest lessons:

1.
2.
3.

Three things I am most grateful for:

1.
2.
3.

Three changes I have made in my life:

1.
2.
3.

What I really want to be acknowledged for:

My advice to myself:

My priorities for the year ahead:

Notes

Notes

Notes

Notes

Notes

Notes

Notes

Notes

Notes

Notes

Notes

Notes

FOR MORE COPIES VISIT OUR WEBSITE

www.getupandgodiary.com

OR CONTACT US ON

info@getupandgodiary.com

Postal address: **Get Up and Go Publications Ltd, Camboline, Hazelwood, Sligo, Ireland F91 NP04.**

For current prices, special offers and postal charges for your region, please refer to the website (www.getupandgodiary.com).

DIRECT ORDER FORM (please complete by ticking boxes)

PLEASE SEND ME:

The Irish Get Up and Go Diary	Year		Quantity	
The Irish Get Up and Go Diary (case bound)	Year		Quantity	
Get Up and Go Diary for Busy Women	Year		Quantity	
Get Up and Go Diary for Busy Women (case bound)	Year		Quantity	
Get Up and Go Young Persons' Diary	Year		Quantity	
Get Up and Go Daily Planner for Busy Women	Year		Quantity	
Get Up and Go Gratitude Journal			Quantity	
Get Up and Go Wallplanner	Year		Quantity	
Get Up and Go Travel Journal			Quantity	
Get Up and Go Genius Journal			Quantity	
Get Up and Go Student Journal (homework journal)	Year		Quantity	
Get Up and Go Heroes (all proceeds to charity)			Quantity	
The Confidence to Succeed (by Donna Kennedy)			Quantity	
			Total number of copies	

I enclose cheque/postal order for (total amount including P+P): ____________________

Name: ____________________

Address: ____________________

Contact phone number: ____________ Email: ____________________

For queries, or to pay by credit card, please contact us on 071 9146717/085 1764297.

2022

January

S	M	T	W	T	F	S
						1
2	3	4	5	6	7	8
9	10	11	12	13	14	15
16	17	18	19	20	21	22
23	24	25	26	27	28	29
30	31					

February

S	M	T	W	T	F	S
		1	2	3	4	5
6	7	8	9	10	11	12
13	14	15	16	17	18	19
20	21	22	23	24	25	26
27	28					

May

S	M	T	W	T	F	S
1	2	3	4	5	6	7
8	9	10	11	12	13	14
15	16	17	18	19	20	21
22	23	24	25	26	27	28
29	30	31				

June

S	M	T	W	T	F	S
			1	2	3	4
5	6	7	8	9	10	11
12	13	14	15	16	17	18
19	20	21	22	23	24	25
26	27	28	29	30		

September

S	M	T	W	T	F	S
				1	2	3
4	5	6	7	8	9	10
11	12	13	14	15	16	17
18	19	20	21	22	23	24
25	26	27	28	29	30	

October

S	M	T	W	T	F	S
						1
2	3	4	5	6	7	8
9	10	11	12	13	14	15
16	17	18	19	20	21	22
23	24	25	26	27	28	29
30	31					

CALENDAR

March

M	T	W	T	F	S
	1	2	3	4	5
7	8	9	10	11	12
14	15	16	17	18	19
21	22	23	24	25	26
28	29	30	31		

April

S	M	T	W	T	F	S
					1	2
3	4	5	6	7	8	9
10	11	12	13	14	15	16
17	18	19	20	21	22	23
24	25	26	27	28	29	30

July

M	T	W	T	F	S
				1	2
4	5	6	7	8	9
11	12	13	14	15	16
18	19	20	21	22	23
25	26	27	28	29	30

August

S	M	T	W	T	F	S
	1	2	3	4	5	6
7	8	9	10	11	12	13
14	15	16	17	18	19	20
21	22	23	24	25	26	27
28	29	30	31			

November

M	T	W	T	F	S
	1	2	3	4	5
7	8	9	10	11	12
14	15	16	17	18	19
21	22	23	24	25	26
28	29	30			

December

S	M	T	W	T	F	S
				1	2	3
4	5	6	7	8	9	10
11	12	13	14	15	16	17
18	19	20	21	22	23	24
25	26	27	28	29	30	31

2023 CALENDAR

JANUARY

S	M	T	W	T	F	S
1	2	3	4	5	6	7
8	9	10	11	12	13	14
15	16	17	18	19	20	21
22	23	24	25	26	27	28
29	30	31				

FEBRUARY

S	M	T	W	T	F	S
			1	2	3	4
5	6	7	8	9	10	11
12	13	14	15	16	17	18
19	20	21	22	23	24	25
26	27	28				

MARCH

S	M	T	W	T	F	S
			1	2	3	4
5	6	7	8	9	10	11
12	13	14	15	16	17	18
19	20	21	22	23	24	25
26	27	28	29	30	31	

APRIL

S	M	T	W	T	F	S
						1
2	3	4	5	6	7	8
9	10	11	12	13	14	15
16	17	18	19	20	21	22
23	24	25	26	27	28	29
30						

MAY

S	M	T	W	T	F	S
	1	2	3	4	5	6
7	8	9	10	11	12	13
14	15	16	17	18	19	20
21	22	23	24	25	26	27
28	29	30	31			

JUNE

S	M	T	W	T	F	S
				1	2	3
4	5	6	7	8	9	10
11	12	13	14	15	16	17
18	19	20	21	22	23	24
25	26	27	28	29	30	

JULY

S	M	T	W	T	F	S
						1
2	3	4	5	6	7	8
9	10	11	12	13	14	15
16	17	18	19	20	21	22
23	24	25	26	27	28	29
30	31					

AUGUST

S	M	T	W	T	F	S
		1	2	3	4	5
6	7	8	9	10	11	12
13	14	15	16	17	18	19
20	21	22	23	24	25	26
27	28	29	30	31		

SEPTEMBER

S	M	T	W	T	F	S
					1	2
3	4	5	6	7	8	9
10	11	12	13	14	15	16
17	18	19	20	21	22	23
24	25	26	27	28	29	30

OCTOBER

S	M	T	W	T	F	S
1	2	3	4	5	6	7
8	9	10	11	12	13	14
15	16	17	18	19	20	21
22	23	24	25	26	27	28
29	30	31				

NOVEMBER

S	M	T	W	T	F	S
			1	2	3	4
5	6	7	8	9	10	11
12	13	14	15	16	17	18
19	20	21	22	23	24	25
26	27	28	29	30		

DECEMBER

S	M	T	W	T	F	S
					1	2
3	4	5	6	7	8	9
10	11	12	13	14	15	16
17	18	19	20	21	22	23
24	25	26	27	28	29	30

2024 CALENDAR

JANUARY

S	M	T	W	T	F	S
	1	2	3	4	5	6
7	8	9	10	11	12	13
14	15	16	17	18	19	20
21	22	23	24	25	26	27
28	29	30	31			

FEBRUARY

S	M	T	W	T	F	S
				1	2	3
4	5	6	7	8	9	10
11	12	13	14	15	16	17
18	19	20	21	22	23	24
25	26	27	28	29		

MARCH

S	M	T	W	T	F	S
					1	2
3	4	5	6	7	8	9
10	11	12	13	14	15	16
17	18	19	20	21	22	23
24	25	26	27	28	29	30
31						

APRIL

S	M	T	W	T	F	S
	1	2	3	4	5	6
7	8	9	10	11	12	13
14	15	16	17	18	19	20
21	22	23	24	25	26	27
28	29	30				

MAY

S	M	T	W	T	F	S
			1	2	3	4
5	6	7	8	9	10	11
12	13	14	15	16	17	18
19	20	21	22	23	24	25
26	27	28	29	30	31	

JUNE

S	M	T	W	T	F	S
						1
2	3	4	5	6	7	8
9	10	11	12	13	14	15
16	17	18	19	20	21	22
23	24	25	26	27	28	29
30						

JULY

S	M	T	W	T	F	S
	1	2	3	4	5	6
7	8	9	10	11	12	13
14	15	16	17	18	19	20
21	22	23	24	25	26	27
28	29	30	31			

AUGUST

S	M	T	W	T	F	S
				1	2	3
4	5	6	7	8	9	10
11	12	13	14	15	16	17
18	19	20	21	22	23	24
25	26	27	28	29	30	31

SEPTEMBER

S	M	T	W	T	F	S
1	2	3	4	5	6	7
8	9	10	11	12	13	14
15	16	17	18	19	20	21
22	23	24	25	26	27	28
29	30					

OCTOBER

S	M	T	W	T	F	S
		1	2	3	4	5
6	7	8	9	10	11	12
13	14	15	16	17	18	19
20	21	22	23	24	25	26
27	28	29	30	31		

NOVEMBER

S	M	T	W	T	F	S
					1	2
3	4	5	6	7	8	9
10	11	12	13	14	15	16
17	18	19	20	21	22	23
24	25	26	27	28	29	30

DECEMBER

S	M	T	W	T	F	S
1	2	3	4	5	6	7
8	9	10	11	12	13	14
15	16	17	18	19	20	21
22	23	24	25	26	27	28
29	30	31